The Power of His Name

The Power of His Name

The Power

Harper & Brothers, Publishers
New York

# of His Name

A Book of Sermons

By ROBERT E. LUCCOCK

Grateful acknowledgment is made to the following for permission to
quote from copyrighted works:

HARCOURT, BRACE AND COMPANY, INC. for lines from the following
works by T. S. Eliot: *Murder in the Cathedral,* copyright 1935 by
Harcourt, Brace and Company, Inc.; *The Cocktail Party,* copyright
1950 by T. S. Eliot; *The Rock,* copyright 1934 by Harcourt, Brace and
Company, Inc.

THE MACMILLAN COMPANY for "The Coming of Christ" by John Masefield, copyright 1920 by John Masefield.

THE NEW YORKER MAGAZINE, INC. for "The Perforated Spirit" by
Morris Bishop, copyright © 1955 by The New Yorker Magazine, Inc.

RINEHART & COMPANY, INC. for "Minor Litany" from *The Selected
Works of Stephen Vincent Benét,* copyright 1940 by Stephen Vincent Benét.

THE VIKING PRESS, INC. for "Midcentury Love Letter" from *The Love
Letters of Phyllis McGinley* by Phyllis McGinley, copyright 1953 by
Phyllis McGinley, orignally printed in The New Yorker.

THE LITERARY TRUSTEES OF WALTER DE LA MARE and THE SOCIETY OF
AUTHORS, London, for "The Listeners" from *The Collected Poems of
Walter de la Mare,* copyright 1920 by Walter de la Mare and pub-
lished in the United States of America by Henry Holt and Company.

Library of Congress catalog card number: 60–8138

To My Mother
From whom I first learned of
the Power of His Name
With Gratitude

CONTENTS

ACKNOWLEDGMENTS

In addition to the publishers and authors' agents listed on the copyright page, the author owes a debt of gratitude to others whose interest and effort have made this book possible.

The sermons on the theme "We would see Jesus" were delivered in another form at the Pastor's School of the Northern California Methodist Conference and at the Ministers' Convocation of the Vermont Congregational Conference. The author is indebted to the generous encouragement of the ministers in these gatherings, and particularly to Bishop Donald Tippett and Myron Herrell of California, and to Max Webster and Harper Welch of Vermont. I am grateful to my secretary Marietta Edmonds for both helpful suggestion and unsparing effort. And most of all my gratitude to my wife Barbara who shared abundantly that the work could be done.

Preface

THE Greeks who once came to Philip at the Passover, saying, "We would see Jesus," have contemporary counterparts. People in every kind of need, sin and fear, doubt and despair, loneliness and anger still come in search of help and hope from Christ. These sermons were preached to congregations that counted many such seekers in their number, their faith often tempered with doubt, their expectation mingled with mistrust. "Lord, I believe; help my unbelief."

It is the purpose of these sermons to help faithful and seeking listeners in their unbelief. The intention of this preaching is to make clear that what God has done in Christ does make a difference to our loneliness, our anxiety, the emptiness of life from which the meaning has fled. It is the hope of the preacher to show how the gospel makes that life-and-death difference, how it overcomes our radical isolation from each other, how it heals our estrangement from God, how it transforms our anxiety into assurance, our alienation into acceptance. Prompting each of these sermons is the wish to speak faith to our unbelief, and to convey trust to our loss of nerve, to enable some listener who has done all he could, to stand yet awhile longer.

The eight sermons that constitute the central portion of the book were preached in a single series during Lent; the three sermons in the title group were given in Advent; and the final three were delivered at Easter, Pentecost, and on Trinity Sunday. It is the author's hope that the gospel in these sermons is the same gospel once delivered to the saints. The task which this preaching called for was to direct that gospel to some of the peculiar and urgent needs of this time, to face the existential questions raised by life in mid-twentieth century. Insofar as possible the traditional terminology of piety has been avoided in favor of language, analogy, symbol, and picture that would arrest the mind and appeal to the imagination of the listener who would reaffirm his faith in a climate of questioning and mistrust.

R.E.L.

Advent: The Power of His Name

I

When the Best We Have Is Not Enough

EMMANUEL

THREE names were given to our Lord in the announcements of his birth as told in the Gospels of Matthew and Luke. In the first chapter of Matthew the angel tells Joseph that his name shall be called *Emmanuel*, which means "God with us." Again, in the same chapter, the angel tells Joseph, "You shall call his name Jesus, for he shall save his people from their sins." In the second chapter of Luke the angel proclaims at Bethlehem, "Unto you is born this day a Saviour who is *Christ* the Lord." From these three names given to our Lord comes the power which he can give to us.

"What's in a name?" we often ask with Romeo. Yet names have often carried great power with them. As Romans in the year 410 A.D., we would have known what was in the name Alaric—the power to strike terror into our hearts. Or as Asians in the late twelfth century, we would have known what was in the name Genghis Khan—the power of barbarous cruelty. And as members of the British fleet at Trafalgar in 1805, we would have known that in the name Lord Nelson lay the power of courage and victory.

Among ancient peoples a name was more than an identification. In a person's name was something of the life and power of the individual himself. The Old Testament priestly blessing, "In the name of the Lord," was a means of conveying a power to the people. Sometimes in the Old Testament the very name signifies the presence of God. When in the New Testament it is said that a person is baptized "into the name of Jesus Christ" it is thought that the person comes under the protection of the bearer of the name. In the same way, if we understand what the names mean that were given to our Lord, we may receive the power which they describe. Truly the power of our Lord is transmitted "through his holy name."

Emmanuel, God with us: In this word is contained the great central meaning of the Incarnation: that God Himself came to the world in Jesus Christ. Consider it in the form of an allegory. A father allowed his children to go on a distant journey to make their home in a far-off country—let us say from the United States to Australia. He gave them his best advice on how to live; he sent along guides to show them the way. But before long they found life in the new land too difficult to manage. Again and again they found themselves in trouble; again and again they failed in one thing after another. Their father sent letters and laws for them to obey. He sent teachers, and he sent men to whom he gave what we would call the power of attorney to manage their affairs for a time. But when left to themselves they always got into the same old difficulties. Somehow all that the father had done was not enough.

Now it is no doubt a vast oversimplification to imply that God could not make up His mind how to help His family or even to suggest that God had not helped His people by His presence, but there is a truth in saying that this is just where the Old Testament leaves us. At this point the father has only two alternatives: he can either leave his children to fare as best they can, or he can go himself out to Australia and help them. When God had done everything that is reported in the Old Testament, in the old covenant, He could either leave His family to die without further help or hope, or He could come and visit them. The gospel tells us that *to the great family of man* God Himself has come in a unique way in Jesus Christ. The gospel is good news that Jesus came full of God's grace and truth, full of His power and His love. From this time forth, and even forevermore, God dwells with us. Why? We shall never know the full answer to that question. But this much we know: against the power of sin the best that man can do is not enough; in the face of death the best that we have is not enough; to save the world from destruction the best that we can accomplish is not enough. We need the help of One who is greater.

Long ago such help did come in the person of a Saviour, who was born in Bethlehem of Judea, crucified on Calvary under Pontius Pilate, and raised from the dead by the power of God. This happened once, historically. But it happens over and over again spiritually as the same God comes to every present situation where the best that we have today is not enough—where the best laws are not enough, the best teaching is not enough, the best examples are not enough—where only God Himself is adequate.

First, there is power in the name Emmanuel for the person who cannot handle the problems of his own life. There is power in a name which tells us that man is not up against these problems in his own strength alone—that God is committed here also. The alcoholic knows this. The person who has fallen into the grip of alcohol and will face the truth about himself knows that the best he has is not enough to defeat the power of liquor. He needs a power greater than himself. These are the first three of the twelve steps of therapy in Alcoholics Anonymous:

1. We admitted that we were powerless over alcohol, that our lives had become unmanageable.
2. We came to believe that a Power greater than ourselves could restore us to sanity.
3. We made a decision to turn our will and our lives over to the care of God, as we understand Him.

But if I were an alcoholic it would not be enough for me to know that this Power exists. I would have to know that this Power can come to me. I would need something more than the belief in God; nearly everyone believes in some kind of Supreme Power or Being. What I need is knowledge that this Power cares about me, is concerned about my being lost in the swamps of drunkenness.

The conviction that the power of God reaches out to me comes most strongly through what God began to do at the manger where he was born whom we call Emmanuel. Is it not like standing on the brink of Niagara Falls watching that tremendous power of water thundering over the cliff, knowing that millions of kilowatt-hours of electric power are right in front of me but none of it to light my way in darkness, none of it to heat my home in the cold, none of it to supply energy for my work, until the power is brought from the falls to the place where I need it? In Jesus Christ the vast resources of God's Niagara are brought to the places where the best that men have is not enough. Which is to say, the alcoholic can know a God who does care, whose power will help.

And not only the alcoholic. In every kind of situation stand men and women whose best is not enough—men and women with burdens too heavy for them to carry, problems too entangled for them to straighten out, anxieties too oppressive for them to bear. Only a power great enough and loving enough to lift what we cannot support, to unsnarl what we cannot figure out, to relieve what we can fight no longer can get us through without disaster. Because of our Lord, Emmanuel, we know of a God to whom we can give the burdens that are too great for the best we have. And trust His loving care to find a way!

J. Middleton Murry tells us how, driven by personal discouragement and sorrow to suicidal despair, he found the way to a new and deeper meaning in existence:

What happened then? If I could tell that I should tell a secret indeed. But a moment came when the darkness of the ocean changed into light, the cold to warmth; when it swept in one great wave over the shores and frontiers of myself, when it bathed me and I was renewed; when the room was filled with a Presence, and I knew I was not alone, that I never could be alone any more; that the universe beyond held no menace; for I was part of it; that in some way for which I had sought in vain so many years, I belonged; and because I belonged I was no longer I, but something different, which could never be afraid in the old ways or cowardly with the old cowardice.[1]

This is the power of His name, Emmanuel—that we belong to Him!

Second, again, there is the power of the name Emmanuel for the person who stands in the desolation left by death. The best that man has is not enough in that moment! What is the gospel for the parents of children who are burned to death in a school fire in Chicago? Is it courage? Friendship? Love? These are all in it. And every parent who walks in that valley wants to hear about God's love. But they want more than that. They want God's love to reach out to them and enfold them in the embrace of eternal love. The best they have of courage, knowledge, friendship, is not enough for the open grave and the empty chair. Only Emmanuel, God with us, tasting of our death, and loving us through death unto everlasting life, is equal to those!

Rufus Jones, Quaker writer and philosopher, tells of going from America to England in July of 1903 and leaving his son Lowell in America. Lowell, ill with diphtheria, had seemed on the road to recovery when his father left for England. A relapse, accompanied by paralysis, set in, and death came. News of this sorrow reached Rufus Jones by cable when his ship docked at Liverpool. But Rufus Jones felt sure, amid the suffering, that for his son Lowell "there was more ahead":

I know now, as I look back across the years, that nothing has carried me up into the life of God, or done more to open out the infinite meaning of love, than the fact that love can span this break of separation, can pass beyond the visible and hold right on across the chasm. The mystic union has not broken and knows no end. Lowell had here only eleven years of happy joyous life. The victory that comes through the long years of struggle in a world full of hard choices could not be his. He was not to have the chance "with toil of heart and knees and hands through the long gorge to the far light" to form his character and to do his life work; but who knows what chances there are for transplanted human worth to bloom, to profit in God's other garden? As certainly as God lives there is more to follow after this brief span of preparation ends.

Yes, "where there is so much love, *there must be more*."[2]

Rufus Jones, in the direct encounter of some luminous moment, came to deep convictions in these matters. For most of us this persuasion that "where there is so much love, there must be more" comes through Jesus Christ our Lord, who took our last enemy, death itself, and defeated him.

Third, there is power in his name Emmanuel for the man whose problems are beyond his skill to handle; power in his name for the one who walks through the valley of the shadow of death; and power in his name for the man who knows despair over the emptiness of life, the loss of meaning so prevalent in our day, the whole pointless disintegration of life into a wasteland of existence. These are the words spoken by the Chorus in T. S. Eliot's *Murder in the Cathedral:*

> God gave us always some reason, some hope;
> but now a new terror has soiled us, which
> none can avert, none can avoid, flowing
> under our feet and over the sky.
>
> Under doors and down chimneys, flowing in
> at the ear and the mouth and the eye.
> God is leaving us, God is leaving us, more
> pang, more pain than birth or death,
> Sweet and cloying through the dark air
> falls the stifling scent of despair.[3]

These lines were written about Thomas à Becket; they might well have been composed for the nuclear and space age, with its anxieties and despair. These are not just the morose ruminations of a melancholy poet: we live in a world of despair, where hope has flickered out, from which, for many people, God seems to have fled and deserted them. If you have any doubt about it, talk to the person who has devoted a lifetime of saving and preparation to educate his children and then finds one day that education is meaningless; talk to the person whose life has gone suddenly to pieces in some kind of senseless wreck; talk to the person for whom years of labor have collapsed in indiscriminate economic ruin;

listen to what scientists are saying about the effect of nuclear testing on our children's children; imagine the consequences if our satellites and missiles were to carry hydrogen warheads aimed at the people of Europe or Asia.

"God gave us always some reason, . . . but now a new terror . . ." To the ever-present personal tensions and uncertainties has been added a universal anxiety. The best we have is not enough for any of these things. Stoic courage we can sometimes manage; even love among the ruins of our personal lives, or the ruin of the world. But what does it mean when the tale is told?

But Emmanuel—God with us! Taking all these things into himself, standing beside us through thick and thin, telling us that life in this darkness does have meaning, that neither personal tragedy nor world disaster can separate us from his love, that though the best we have is not enough, the best he has is thrown into the situation for our sake. This makes all the difference. God with us! With you and with me—in our sickness, in our fears, at our death. Explain it? Who can explain it? But we feel it in the power of his name who came to the world in the birth of a child at Bethlehem:

> I know not how that Bethlehem's Babe
> Could in the Godhead be;
> I only know the Manger Child
> Has brought God's life to me.

II

God Helps Those Who Cannot Help Themselves

JESUS

"GOD helps them that help themselves" is one of the aphorisms of Benjamin Franklin. Its truth is obvious: we cannot sit around and wait for God to do something for us that He expects us to do for ourselves. On the other hand, it requires to be said that God does not help everyone who helps himself, particularly when he is helping himself to something he ought not to have. Nor does God's help always come in the way we expect it. But with the approach of Christmas we become aware of an opposite truth of far greater consequence, namely: *God helps those who cannot help themselves*. Much we might say to qualify that. But this truth lies very close to the heart of what Christmas and the Incarnation are all about: that God has come to help us *most* where we can help ourselves *least*—in dealing with the fact of sin.

The name Jesus means literally "The Lord is salvation." Matthew explains its meaning further by reporting that the angel of the Annunciation instructed Joseph to call his child *Jesus*—because he will save his people from their sins. This is the power of his name, that through Jesus whom we call the Christ we can be delivered from the power and bondage of sin, something we cannot do in our own power.

I wonder if there is any way to suggest what good news this is? We are not accustomed to worrying much about our sins, as long as they don't get us into trouble with the law. This news may not seem quite as good to us as it did to the angel who first announced it over Bethlehem fields, largely because it has come to seem almost irrelevant. But it is nothing less than the good news of new life.

You might imagine yourself lying in a hospital, waiting to die, having been told that you suffer from a fatal disease. You are disconsolate with all the anguish and fear of death, when a doctor comes and says to you, "We know of a way to cure your disease; you will not die from this." This would be good news of new life, worthy to be sung by angelic hosts in the heavens.

You might imagine yourself adrift on a life raft far out in angry seas, having no hope that anyone will come before you drown. And then in the darkness—a light, a ship, a rescue! That too would be good news of new life, something for angels to sing about in your heavens.

No less than the good news of healing from mortal disease, or rescue from drowning, is the good news that God will save you from your sin. The doctor who makes the healing for your disease possible and the captain who sails his ship to your life raft are your saviors. They come to save you from a peril from which you cannot save yourself. So Christian faith believes that Jesus comes to save men and women in the peril of sin, which biblical faith has always diagnosed as the greatest peril of all, from which men cannot save themselves.

But suppose you do not suffer from a fatal sickness. How pointless for a doctor to say, "We can cure your disease!" You would say to him, "What disease? Aren't you talking to the wrong man, doctor? I feel fine. I can take care of myself. I'll send for you if I need you." Suppose instead of being out on a life raft in the middle of the Atlantic you are home safe in your bed. It doesn't concern you particularly where the captain sails his ship or shines his light in the night. You're perfectly safe. It becomes a question then of whether you need a Saviour, or whether you actually believe yourself to be in mortal danger from sin. And this, of course, all depends on what you mean by sin, on whether you take sin seriously, and whether you can do anything about it yourself. Ultimately it depends on whether Jesus Christ can do anything about it.

So here we are, back again at that ugly word about which the Bible has so much to say and which we all find so difficult, and sometimes infuriating, to understand: sin! What is it?

Biblical faith, and particularly the faith of the New Testament, has always looked upon sin as something far more serious than a catalogue of immoralities. You commit adultery with your neighbor, you are cruel to your mother and father, you steal money from the company where you work, you deliberately lie about something, you destroy some of your neighbor's property—these are sins. You are not to take them lightly. Moreover, Jesus drove the idea of sin inward, making it an affair of the mind and heart: you look on a woman lustfully, you are angry with your brother, your prayers are full of hypocrisy, you pass by someone in need because he is not of your race, you leave the cries of the hungry, the thirsty, the lonely unanswered—these are sins, and Christian faith takes them most seriously.

But Christian faith is troubled by something more serious than any of these: that man, *who was created in the image of God, spoils that image.* This is sin, that man, made in the image of God, makes himself into the kind of person who can do all these things. When we look at Jesus Christ we see the measure by which we have spoiled the image, the distance that we have fallen from being the creatures God intended us to be. Looking at Jesus is like looking into a perfect mirror; he reflects by his goodness every flaw and imperfection in ourselves. Jesus is the representative man by whom we can measure ourselves before the face of God. No matter how good, or how righteous, or how respectable we imagine ourselves to be, when we compare even our best, to say nothing of our worst, with Christ, we see how marred and broken a thing we have made out of life. And this is what Christian faith takes most seriously!

These are the two great commandments of biblical faith: You shall love the Lord your God with all your heart and mind and strength, and you shall love your neighbor as yourself. But when we hold ourselves up to this measuring rod, we see how we fail. Who of us loves God with *all* his *heart?* Much of the time we love other things more than God: our way of life, our comforts and securities. Who of us loves his neighbor as he loves himself? Much of the time we love our privileges and our advantages more than we love our neighbor. Now if you protest that this is human nature, and that these are counsels of perfection, Christian faith answers, Precisely! We are human, and they are counsels of perfection, and this is exactly what we are talking about. But once in a while a man does give himself in heroic love for a neighbor. Once in a while a man does show his love for God far beyond the ordinary limits of devotion. He loves God with every ounce of devotion in his soul. Then we see what life ought to be all the time, not just once in a while. When we look at Christ, we are brought to shame by what he shows us in ourselves.

Blessed are the pure in heart? But who is wholly pure in heart? Our motives are always alloyed with considerations of what is prudent as well as what is pure.

Seek first the Kingdom of God? But is this what we think of first in making our decisions?

Inasmuch as you do it unto the least of Christ's brothers? The persecuted, ill-treated, hungry, lonely, the prisoner—do we think of these people as we think of ourselves?

Love your enemy? Do we really love our enemy, turning him the other cheek, praying for those who spit on us and push us around?

The closer we come to Jesus, the more we realize how we have defaced the image of God that is in us. Of course, this whole argument assumes that God takes His creation seriously, that it is no small thing to have created man in His own image, and breathed His own Spirit into our souls. Naturally, if we think that God takes a casual, indulgent attitude toward the commandments that we love Him and that we love our neighbor, that it really doesn't make very much difference whether we obey them or not, then, of course, sin is not a very serious affair. To anyone who only casually regards the image of God that is in him, it is meaningless to talk seriously about sin. How does one explain light to a man who has been blind from birth, or music to a person who has always been deaf? What does one say about "home" to a person who has grown up in a concentration camp? Neither can one explain the forgiveness of God to one who has no lively sense of sin, and so no experience of the overwhelming love of God.

But the closer we come to Christ, the more we realize the precious worth of a human soul with its wonderful capacity to respond to the love which is at the heart of creation. And the more precious we discover life to be, the more terrible does the fact of human sin become. Perhaps we may see it better by analogy. I have a cup in my hand. At first glance it looks like any other cup—and any other nineteen-cent cup from the "five and ten" would serve the same purpose. If I were to drop it, the consequent breakage would be unimportant. It would be just a broken cup. In other words, I do not take the cup very seriously. But suppose this cup were a piece of matchless Limoges china, perfect in texture, translucent in its luster, a creation of rare beauty, not to be replaced anywhere. To anyone who knows and loves fine china the destruction would be shocking *because of the value of what was broken*. Suppose we were to care about the souls of men in a way comparable to the way lovers of china would care about the Limoges cup in my hand.

But now suppose I deliberately smash this cup on the floor. That is sin! Not that I have broken the cup, but that I have broken the image of God in myself in the way that I broke the cup. Just as you are shocked at this defacement, the person who knows and loves the image of God in a human soul is most seriously and painfully disturbed by the defacement of life that is sin. The breaking of the image of God disturbs us because through the love of Christ we know what a human soul is worth.

Human souls are not manufactured and distributed through some celestial Woolworth's! We were bought at a far greater price. "And you shall call his name Jesus, for he shall save his people from their sins." Jesus Christ, born in Bethlehem, crucified under Pontius Pilate, and raised from the dead by the power of God, can save us from the power of sin by showing us that we do sin, that we do break the image of God in which we are created, and that our love falls short of the glory of God. This is the first step in salvation: knowing that we need a Saviour, a Saviour to heal our souls that are as broken as that piece of china is broken from the perfect image in which it was made.

Jesus Christ can also save us from the power of sin by turning the hardness of our hearts to love. Seeing Jesus forgive the woman taken in adultery, Jesus in the home of Mary and Martha, Jesus gathering the children to his arms, Jesus lifting Peter up out of sin and remorse, Jesus telling of the good Samaritan and the prodigal son, Jesus forgiving his tormentors—these all move us to turn away from sin, for they show us what life ought to be, and move us with love for such a life. In such love we feel a glory and a power to check the power of sin. Jesus, whose name means "The Lord is salvation," shows us how we sin; he shows us also the wonder of God's love translated into human love. His is the gift of a transformed heart—not all the way, and not always. But the love of Jesus brings us nearer to the love of God, and redeems some measure of the life of the world.

But Jesus Christ does more even than that. Not only does Jesus bring us to the love of God; he brings God's love to the very heart of our sin. In the preceding chapter we spoke of the family who had gone to live in the far country and who kept getting into trouble, to whom the father sent messengers, letters, assistance of every kind, and to whom he finally had to go himself. What we did not say there, but which needs to be said with emphasis now, is that the principal trouble these people had was not with the environment, or with accidents—it was with themselves! They were their own worst enemies. Sin was the most serious problem they had, the problem they could do least about. They could forgive each other the injuries they had inflicted on one another; they could excuse and overlook each other's mistakes. What they could not do was to forgive the sin which was injury done to their father's hope, trust, and love. Only their father could do that. He did it by coming out to them. Only God can forgive sin, because the defacement of the image of God and the breaking of His commandments of love are sins against Him, and only the one sinned against can forgive the sinner. Until we know that God does forgive us we are helplessly and hopelessly trapped in despair—that is, if we take the reality of the goodness of God's creation seriously.

But Jesus Christ does come to bring God's love. His coming, when we face it with vigorous and unflinching imagination, turns us back from sin. We call this turning back *repentance*. It is the one thing God commands us to do. He will do the rest. For everyone who turns from his sin, truly seeking to be saved, God can do what none of us could ever do: put the broken pieces of life together again.

J. Colwell tells us this parable: Many years ago there was a great famine of water in a town in the south of France. It was a hot summer; no rain fell for months, and as the people always suffered from the want of water, this dry hot season greatly increased their sufferings, and many of them died. A few miles away from the town was a range of hills; in the hills were some beautiful springs of water, but the labor and expense of bringing the water from the springs to the town was so great that very little of it could be brought. In this town lived a young man whom we shall call Jean. He was industrious and good, and was shortly to be married to a beautiful young woman whom he dearly loved. But all at once the marriage was put off, the young man began to go about in old clothes, took very little to eat, gave up his pleasant home, and went to live in a garret, and in short, became a thorough miser. He went to bed in the dark to save candles, begged other people's cast-off clothing, and very soon became changed from a blithe and happy young man into a wretched-looking old one. His charming bride-to-be forgot him and married another man. The children called him names in the streets, and everybody shunned his house. After many years of wretchedness he died. When his relatives went to search his room, they found him almost wasted to a skeleton, and all his furniture sold, while the old man's body was lying upon a heap of straw. Under his head they found a will. And only then did it become known that in that dreadful summer forty years ago Jean had been so saddened by the suffering of the people—especially of the children—for want of water that he had given up his young bride, his pleasant home, and his happy prospects to devote himself day and night all through the weary years to working and saving, so that the people might have the beautiful water brought to them from the distant springs in the hillside. How everybody blessed that old man! A reservoir was made in the hills, pipes were laid under the ground, and the water was brought into the town so freely that its inhabitants never thirsted again. The old man did not create the water, neither did he make the people thirst; he simply brought the living water and the dying people together, and he sacrificed himself to do it.[1]

That is how Jesus saves us from the power of sin. He did not create God's love or mercy; those great springs of blessings were and always are in the great heart of God. He did not make men sinful and sad so that they needed those things; but he brought these springs of love and blessing down to the men who were dying for the need of them. He is the channel through which God's love comes to us.

Sin is a serious matter, so serious that God suffered this much on account of it. How can we but do the same? But when we do, we find that God has done for us what we could not do for ourselves—taken away our sin, and made all things new. The power of his name, Jesus—the Lord is salvation.

III

God's Gift to a World That Has Everything

IN THE Christmas story told in Luke's Gospel, the angel proclaims from Bethlehem skies: "Unto you is born a Saviour who is Christ the Lord." Thus a third name was given to our Lord: *Christ*.

The name Christ is a Greek translation, "Christos," of the Hebrew word "Messiah," meaning literally *the Anointed One*. When the Christian Community came to believe that Jesus of Nazareth, born in Bethlehem, crucified under Pontius Pilate, and raised from the dead by the power of God, was the long-expected Messiah of the prophecy, they gave to him the name *Christ*. Before long the name became inseparably attached to Jesus—Jesus Christ —so that what had originally been a title very soon came to be used by the followers of the risen Jesus as a proper name for their Lord. From this they came to be known as Christians, for they believed that Jesus had come in fulfillment of Old Testament prophecy. This conviction still marks the difference between Christians and Jews. It is not for the Christians to say what God's intentions are concerning the Jews. Sufficient for us to know that there is power in the name Christ, for we believe that in Christ, God has visited and redeemed His people. This is our faith: *The Christ that was born in Bethlehem God anointed to redeem the life of the world.* It makes a point of lively theological debate whether God anointed Jesus before his birth or at his birth, his baptism, his transfiguration, or his resurrection. To the meaning of Christmas these are,

30

however, quite irrelevant questions. In the full light and power of the resurrection, and in the company of the risen Lord, Christians came to the unshakable conviction that in Jesus Christ God had fulfilled His promises to send a Wonderful Counselor, the Prince of Peace, to be with us.

At the heart of Christian faith is the trust that God has sent a Saviour to a world having everything that human ingenuity could conceive, but lacking anything to cleanse and purify all that we have. At the heart of Christian faith is the conviction that God has sent a Redeemer to a world without guidance to direct its possessions into saving, healing, redeeming purposes. So, in the time appointed, to a world which had everything except a Saviour, God gave a Saviour, who is Christ the Lord. Admittedly we are using the language of metaphor here to describe the mystery of the Incarnation, a reality that no words can fully contain. If the language of the personal, purposeful intention of God's deliberately anointing Jesus to be the world's Redeemer is baffling, one may still come at the truth by recognizing that Jesus Christ somehow represents the way of peace on earth, good will among men, without which our world is lost, and that in loyal obedience to his Spirit, our existence can be redeemed from death to life, from destruction to peace. What Christian faith is saying through all the figures and symbols of its speech, its art, its music, is that Christ not only reveals but makes available to all who will receive it the divine power to destroy evil.

In one sense, this power is not yet fully manifest. Faith looks toward the day when God's Kingdom will come in all its fullness. By comparison with familiar things truth stands forth. Have you ever suffered through a stifling, sultry summer day, nearly prostrate with the heat and then seen a great storm boil up out of the west in the afternoon—enormous thunderheads, with their warning sound of the power within them, the flash of lightning across the darkening sky, the gusts of wind whirling down as earnest of what follows? The power to shake off the grip of oppressive heat is unmistakably revealed in these signs; a great storm promises to break overhead. But the time has not come. So we may think of Christ's coming and of his challenge to the powers of darkness. He has demonstrated God's power in the face of evil. His Kingdom promises to come; we have already seen evidences of it in Jesus' own life, and in the remarkable witness of the faith and of the Church across the ages. The truth is that the kingdoms of this world shall become the Kingdom of our Lord and His Christ. The reign of Christ, the Anointed One, shall yet come in all fullness.

In another sense, the redeeming power of the Saviour is already present. It has come in Jesus Christ. It is available through the Risen Lord. We experience it in the company of the Church. To change the figure of speech, it is as though men would one day reclaim a wilderness region for life, would make a desert bloom, would build homes, churches, schools, and parks. The heat, the light—the power to do these things—has already been brought out to the wilderness. Men can even now use it to illumine the darkness, to bring irrigation to a dry and thirsty land. In the same way Christ the Saviour has already visited and redeemed his people. The Saviour's power has already touched us. When we receive him, life can be changed and transformed even now.

We see this truth set forth in the high drama of the Christmas story itself. The Wise Men are our representatives in the story of Jesus' birth. They are the men who had everything their world could bestow of wealth, power, and knowledge. Yet they brought all these things to the manger of the Christ Child—and then they returned to their own country by another way. In the symbol of their wealth, their power, and their knowledge being redeemed by the coming of Christ there is moving effect for us. We are twentieth-century men who have everything our world can give. We have ample wealth, we have a kind of limitless power, we have knowledge almost to harness the elemental force of creation. Our wealth, our power, our knowledge can also be transformed by the power of Christ, so that we return to former life by another way. Indeed it is precisely to do these things that God anointed Jesus as the Christ, the Saviour of the world.

In Masefield's Whitsuntide drama, *The Coming of Christ*,[1] the three Wise Men speak of the power of their possessions, and at the same time of the need to have their possessions redeemed and their lives transformed. Listen to each one as he speaks in turn. The first is Balthasar:

> I am King Balthasar the Fierce,
> Whom all men dread yet dare not curse,
> My nerves are iron, my heart stone;
> My subjects live for war alone,
> War as I bid, until I choose.
> My subjects are the tools I use,
> My slaves who buckle on my steel,
> And face to front and come to heel
> In war, from boyhood till they die.
>
> I know my rule of blood must cease;
> I know that it is based on wrong,
> On callousness among the strong,
> On cruelty. The bloody deeds
> Which I have cast abroad as seeds,
> Now rise in such a crop of fear
> That in the lightest sound I hear
> My victims coming; so I seek
> This Saviour-King of whom men speak.

Can the fierce power of our heads and our hands be redeemed by Christ? It is our fear that unless such power is redeemed it will bring our destruction.

These are the words of Norman Cousins:

Leading nuclear physicists today believe that the United States and Soviet Russia, between them, now possess more than the number of fission and fusion bombs required to burn off all forms of life on this planet. This fact should be considered against the background of warnings by responsible leaders of government who have served public notice that nothing would be held back in the event of war. . . .

If war should come, it will be only superficially a war between nations. Essentially, it will be a war against God. For it is the work of

God and not of man alone that is now in jeopardy. The precariously balanced conditions that make life on this planet possible—not solely human life but life in general—those conditions can now be smashed or altered. Man's works of art, his cities, his cathedrals, his homes are palpable, personally replaceable. But his genes and his basic nature—these belong to a higher design and are not his to expunge or assail. Yet this can be the effect of his present perilous journey.[2]

It must be the world's hope that this power can be redeemed by Christ, that by his Spirit we shall find a grace, a wisdom, and a holy purpose to do what needs to be done to transform our power from destruction to peace. For the world that has the unlimited power for the life or death of humanity God gave His Son to redeem this power for Himself and His purposes.

Hear now the words of Gaspar, the second of the Magi:

> I am Gaspar, the wealthy; I trade in my ships to the West.
> All gold and all goods and all glories are mine to enjoy.
> All the beauty that skill has created or greed has possest,
> All are mine, and the men I employ,
> All are mine from the pride of their toil
>   to the dreams of their rest.
>
> I govern all markets, I usure my gold to all Kings,
> Command all the men of the sea, of the mine,
>   of the field,
> Set thinkers to conquer disease, or to fashion men wings
> And wealth is the weapon I wield
> As I live at my ease in a palace of beautiful things.
>
> I must die, leaving all I possess, losing
>   all my schemes,
> All the joy of my knowledge of men, all my
>   skill with the net,
> All the glory of bringing to market the
>   things of my dreams,
> All the roar of my mills on the streams:
> I shall quake as my debtors have quaked,
>   and my life will be debt.

> They say that a King will be born who will
> end this despair. . . .
> They say that this coming will make even
> death to be fair.
> O comfort more precious than gold.
> I seek for this monarch, and cry for his
> help, being old.

Our vast wealth and all our possessions—could they be released to lift up mankind from poverty and oppression? This money is not being so released. In a recent year in the United States 2.2 per cent of the personal income was given to religious bodies, to welfare activities, and all private education and research. But in the same year 5.2 per cent of personal income was spent for alcoholic beverages and tobacco—more than twice as much spent for alcohol and tobacco as for all welfare and religious activity. Our wealth—unredeemed!

These are the words of the third of the Magi, Melchior:

> I am that Melchior who seek
> Below the pit, above the peak,
> To find what *is*, beyond what seems,
> I seek for truth in things and dreams,
> In Wise Men's myths and old wives' tales
> With all my strength, yet naught avails.
>
> I fasted like a starving beast,
> Breaking my flesh that my soul might feast;
> I tried the wisdoms of the East;
>
> I tried the madness of the West,
> The quietude and the unrest:
> No way was Truth, no way was best.
> O marvelous Master, let me find
> Some link that will forever bind
> Our minds to an eternal mind.
>
> Let me not die in all my yearning
> For Hope in Life and none discerning;

> Grant that this holy planet burning
> May, as men say, foretell the birth
> Of one who comes to save the earth
> As God and King in man alive.

Could our knowledge of technology, our knowledge of each
other, and our knowledge of life itself be redeemed by the
Anointed One of God? Shining high above our city on these
Advent nights is a cross formed by lighted windows in the tele-
phone building. This symbol spreads its effect over all beneath it—
an effect of beauty and holy reminder. But far beyond the beauty
of this cross is its symbolic meaning: the way and the Spirit of the
Saviour imprinted upon the ways of our whole civilization repre-
sented by the communication center for our whole structure of
life. This symbol of Christ shining forth *from within* the life of
our civilization proclaims the truth of Christmas and the Incarnation: that the people who have everything, symbolized by the
towers of our knowledge, have now in Christ the gift of a love to
save our knowledge from futility. O Christ, if thou couldst send us
back to the realms where we live all the time by another way, then
thou wouldst be the Christ unto us!

"Messages from the Invisible Universe" is the title which Arthur
C. Clarke gives to an article in the *New York Times*. This is the
first paragraph:

For thousands of years men have looked up at the sun, moon and
stars—and believed that they saw the universe. Within the last decade,
we have discovered that they saw—even with the greatest telescopes—
only *one* universe, and that another exists, invisible to the eye. This is
the universe revealed not by light, but by the millionfold longer waves
of radio. It has been a revelation indeed; today's astronomers are like
blind men who have suddenly been granted the gift of sight. It will be
years before they can fully interpret what they observe—or rather what
their wonderful new instrument, the radio-telescope, observes for them.

Radio-telescopes are like great inverted bowls, sometimes 250
feet in diameter, turned upward toward the heavens to receive the

radio impulses coming in from interstellar space. The most amazing and mysterious signals yet heard are not thought to come from intelligent creatures like ourselves, if indeed we are intelligent. They are thought rather to be the impulses generated by one of the most awe-inspiring phenomena ever discovered—nothing less than a head-on collision of two island universes or galaxies. But the article closed with these words of hope for what man may some day discover when radio-telescopes can be built out in space beyond the interference of the world's atmosphere:

Clear of the man-made interference which now drenches our planet, they will be able to gather far more energy than today's antenna systems and, what is equally important, will be able to focus with much greater precision upon selected small regions of space. We can be certain that these vast instruments will bring us nearer to a true understanding of our universe; and we can hope that, one day, they will tell us that *we are not alone* in its immensity.[3]

The hope here is that the instruments may reveal other life in the universe. But our imagination lifts those words infinitely higher to another hope. Would it not be true to say that in other dimensions of reality the birth of Christ comes to the receptive heart as a message from the invisible heart of creation, which we call God, telling us that we are not alone in the universe, that God is with us to save us from sin and death, and to redeem all the life that we give Him from futility?

We Would See Jesus

IV

"In a Raveled World, Love Endures"

CHRIST, THE REDEEMER OF
LIFE'S LOST MEANING

IN THE twelfth chapter of the Gospel of John it is reported that some Greeks came to Philip at the Feast of the Passover saying, "We would see Jesus." These nameless Greeks stand at the head of an unnumbered procession of people stretching across the ages from that day until now who have come to Christian disciples saying, "We would see Jesus." You and I are in the procession. Those Greeks spoke for us. The writer of the Gospel does not tell us what the Greeks were seeking. We know what multitudes have sought who followed them.

What an assemblage has come in quest of a teacher, one to give direction and control in the social, personal, and moral affairs of life. Some journey through the fearsome wilderness of sin saying, "We would see Jesus as forgiving God." Others come in hope that through Jesus they might talk with God in God's own tongue. We see the lonely who sought the blessing of a beloved community where Jesus was Master. With them stand anxious souls, full of dread and desperate to find peace. There are the frightened strong ones of the earth looking for a Saviour of the world. Far from least either in number or in need walk that endless company who in shadowed valleys seek the risen Lord.

Perhaps for more than any other reason multitudes in our world come because *they have lost life's meaning*. (So it might have been with those first Greeks, inquiring for Jesus less out of curiosity than out of a deep need to find new meaning and greater purpose for life, in want of One who could redeem the senseless vacancy at life's center.) With lives turned hollow, lack-luster, empty of significance they search for a Redeemer to fill this void. These legions of folk do not say, "We would see Jesus," but they seek for meanings which Jesus alone can give. They too are counted with the Greeks.

Some come in their loss of love. In an essay descriptively entitled "In a Raveled World, Love Endures," Robert Gorham Davis points out that the best novels written since World War II reveal a "great loneliness and a need for love among the people whom they depict. They attempt to make very simple human relationships bear almost impossibly heavy social and philosophical burdens. Love has a special character and urgency. It is the only recourse against radical isolation, against a terrifying sense of meaninglessness."[1] The radical isolation in which these fictional characters find themselves accurately reflects the real loneliness in the world of our time. The tragedy of life for so many is in the absence of love. They neither get beyond themselves through love, nor are loved in sufficient measure against loneliness and radical isolation. Life becomes a frightful nothingness when love is lost. They would see Jesus that his love, expressed in simple human relationships, might restore the meaning.

Others come in their loss of identity and self-esteem. Our world buries the vast majority of its people in an impersonal obscurity. Norman Cousins has put it this way:

Impersonality is epidemic. It is almost as though we feared direct contact, almost as though the soul of man had become septic.

If a man becomes ill he hardly hangs up his hat in the doctor's office before he is placed before a whole battery of machines and testing devices. The traveled road is not between the mind of the diagnostician and the heart of the patient, but between the clinic and the laboratory.

If a man submits himself for a job he is seen not as a personality but as a fit subject for various tests which presumably have more to do with ascertaining his worth than the human responses which may figure largely in the work he is called upon to do.

If a man builds a house he no longer participates in a wonderful joint enterprise with his neighbors but in a juggling contest with figures, and he may not see his neighbors from one year to the next. The house itself may be shiny and functional, but not a thing is known about the people who made it.

If a man wishes to help needy people he generally does it not on a man-to-man basis but through an agency; and his contribution becomes a statistic rather than a strand in a lifeline thrown to a recognizable being.[2]

Morris Bishop has caught the sense of lifelessness in his lines called "The Perforated Spirit."

> The fellows up in Personnel
> They have a set of cards on me.
> The sprinkled perforations tell
> My individuality.
>
> And what am I? I am a chart
> Upon the cards of IBM.
> The secret places of the heart
> Have little secrecy for them.
>
> It matters not how much I prate
> They punch with punishment the scroll.
> The files are masters of my fate,
> They are the captains of my soul.
>
> Monday my brain began to buzz,
> I was in agony all night.
> I found out what the trouble was,[3]
> They had my paper clip too tight.

Perforated spirits and soulless identities are not satisfied. They come seeking escape out of the mass pattern which the ad man and the machine have created, saying, "We would see Jesus, that he may make some more satisfying personal sense out of life."

Others are numbered with the Greeks who seek a Redeemer because they have lost the reason for living. In a convalescent home some time ago an invalid lady spoke for a multitude when she said, "I don't understand why the good Lord spares me this way. I'm not needed; I'm not wanted. Nobody cares whether I live or die." That feeling is scarcely restricted to convalescent homes. We live to increasingly advanced years, but our strength and health outstay our usefulness. Something purposeful to do, somewhere to be needed, some emblem or commitment to which life is sworn, some glad hope to be cherished—these are the heroic dimensions of life. We all know persons who have discovered no place where they are really needed, who find nothing of substance to do, whose heraldry has been all beaten out of them, and in whose hearts the ashes of hope are cold. They would see Jesus, that he might give them reason for life.

Again, many would see Jesus in order to get off the merry-go-round where life has lost its expectancy of anything new that could give it a glory. How many would say with Marcus Aurelius: "Up and down, to and fro, round and round: this is the monotonous and meaningless rhythm of the universe. A man of ordinary mental powers who has reached the age of forty has experienced everything that has been, is, and is to come." Some would see Jesus to find if perchance *he* has broken out of the treadmill into green pastures of discovery and highlands of new adventure.

Beyond these, somewhere far down in the dim subconscious mind is the dark shadow which modern man flees, or faces only with the greatest courage. What does the whole process mean, the creation which has been groaning in travail together until now, since man has irretrievably seized power to destroy all life upon the earth? Has man put God into checkmate? To whom shall he go to confirm life's final meanings beyond the present possibility —except to Jesus? And many wonder if even Jesus has the answer.

Wondering this, those in greatest need come seeking Jesus because their sense of God has grown dim. "In the heart of every man," said H. G. Wells, "is a god-shaped place." But when this god-shaped place is empty, it leaves a longing in the heart that nothing else can satisfy. As one man wrote out of first-hand experience:

It is an awful moment when the soul begins to find that the props on which it has blindly rested so long are, many of them, rotten, and begins to suspect them all; when it begins to feel the nothingness of many of the traditional opinions which have been received with implicit confidence, and in that horrible insecurity begins also to doubt whether there be anything to believe at all. It is an awful hour—let him who has passed through it say how awful—when this life has lost its meaning, and seems shrivelled into a span, when the grave appears to be the end of all, human goodness nothing but a name, and the sky above this universe a dead expanse, black with the void from which God Himself has disappeared.

This is the final abyss of despair. Here we come into dreadful night. Who can endure this despair? More, who can redeem it? We would see Jesus.

"In a raveled world, love endures." In picturesque phrase this contemporary word reiterates the truth of Christian faith: Love never ends. Love can redeem the void that is left when common meanings of life have fled. Suppose we allow this whole need to come to focus in one man, to discover if we can how Jesus Christ might be his Redeemer. Here is a real person, his situation harder than some, but essentially like that of millions. If the gospel has no real answer for this man, it has no real word for any of us:

Of frail health, although he had overcome a disfiguring handicap with remarkable courage, he lived alone. His gracious wife who had tenderly cared for him through the years was dead. They had no children. His job scarcely more than routine, he might have dropped out on any morning and have been easily replaced. Neither in a family nor as part of any other community of people did this life serve a purpose that gave sense or significance beyond the lonely drudgery of mere existence. How could Christ redeem a soul in such shadow?

First, to every soul who has lost faith or hope or love from his life, the gospel's first word is this: *You are not alone for God is with you!* To be sure, this will have to be demonstrated either through God's incarnation in human love, or through the I-Thou relationship of prayer, or through the enlargement of himself by outreach to a community greater than himself. But the Christian good news is that this can be done. As Jesus was about to step out into the night of Gethsemane he said to his disciples, "The hour is coming when you will leave me alone; yet I am not alone, for the Father is with me." These words were proven in the experience of that very night. God's presence with Jesus in the garden, at his arrest, and through all that followed when the whole meaning of his life seemed to be buried in the crash of hopes, redeemed the disaster to love. Jesus was not abandoned in senseless waste. God was with him, turning his suffering love into atonement and a redeeming love for all who come by the same lonely way.

God was present with Jesus in such a way that he could say, "I am in the Father and the Father is in me." It has appeared to the eyes of faith that God Himself was in Jesus. So when this Galilean whom men call Master says, "I come to seek and to save that which was lost . . . and I will be with you always," he is declaring in himself the coming of Almighty God into the human scene, and coming all the way down through the human scene to one lonely man in his unmeaning void. When we meet Christ it is a divine encounter, and the very fact that God does stand present with this forlorn man in his need endows the man's life with a dignity and nobility that redeems the spiritual vacuum. God is in Christ transforming every presence to which the risen and living Lord may come.

Who of us does not stand baffled before the towering mysteries of life? His authority is untested who has not himself heard the good news of God, yet confessed, "Such knowledge is too wonderful for me; it is high, I cannot attain it." The gospel explains very little. But it changes all things. It brings the endowment of courage. In the Old Testament God says to Joshua, "I will not fail you or forsake you. Be strong and very courageous." If God will not fail us, surely here is the source of all courage, changing despair to hope; sorrow to joy; death to life.

Perhaps only in the language of pictures and symbols can we apprehend what this coming means. A parable told by Herbert

Farmer will suggest the height and depth of what God's coming means in personal terms:

> Conceive a child lying alone and in agony in a garret. There is no one at hand to help. There will never be anyone at hand to help. There is just agony, loneliness, lovelessness. So conceived the thing is hideously chill and depressing. Now conceive a mother present, bending over the child, entering into its suffering, surrounding it with an atmosphere of love, and receiving from it looks of love and gratitude in return. The picture has now become an entirely different thing. There is no less pain, no less poverty; yet, taken as a whole, the situation is now markedly less revolting and more satisfying.

The circumstances in that picture remain burdened with pain, but there is present now a beauty and a grace and love that redeem the darkness. In whatever dreariness life brings, I think of God so present in my situation.

Phyllis McGinley's sonnet "Midcentury Loveletter" has about it an inspired beauty but somehow a chilling sadness suggestive of the aloneness and the isolation in which modern life leaves so many.

> Stay near me, speak my name. Oh, do not wander
> By a thought's span, heart's impulse, from the light
> We kindle here. You are my sole defender
> (As I am yours) in this precipitous night,
> Which over earth, till common landmarks alter,
> Is falling, without stars, and bitter cold.
> We two have but our burning selves for shelter.
> Huddle against me. Give me your hand to hold.
>
> So might two climbers lost in mountain weather
> On a high slope and taken by a storm,
> Desperate in the darkness, cling together
> Under one cloak and breathe each other warm.
> Stay near me. Spirit, perishable as bone,
> In no such winter can survive alone.[4]

This is a beautiful picture of our need for human love and the power of that love. In a raveled world love alone can save us from a death-in-life. But these lines are also a desperate midcentury cry of those who have no God, and for whom human love is not enough. "We have but our burning selves for shelter." No! says Christian faith. In the darkness of our winter comes Christ saying, You do not need to face this midcentury or any midcentury alone. In a raveled world my love endures.

Second, the gospel has a word to all who find their lives in a senseless vacuum: "He that loses his life for my sake shall find it." Wherever men and women have come close enough really to see Jesus, they have miraculously found themselves in new relationships with people, out of which they have found new meaning in their own lives. Wherever men and women did see Jesus in truth and reality the immediate and obvious change that occurred was to affect their touch and ties with lives standing next to their own. How many there were on the pages of scripture: a woman of the streets, a tax gatherer, fishermen, soldiers. By a chance meeting with a woman at a well, the pale between Jew and Samaritan was lifted. By a dream which he would not have had but for Jesus, Peter was provoked to call nothing unclean which God has created. Understandable though it is that our friend should lose his life's meaning, it is first and foremost because he turned in upon himself. This, but for the grace of God, is what we all do. But to see Jesus is to turn out into the enfolding relationships of a brotherhood whose members claim the same Father and Creator. In Jesus we discover who our brothers are.

During a recent Christmas season a story appeared in the newspapers whose meaning meets us on a level far above its simple facts. Mrs. Elizabeth Steigerwald Etzl was reunited with her sixteen-year-old son Hansie, whom she had not seen since 1944, when he was five years old. During all those years Mrs. Etzl had followed the trail which finally led to her identification of a boy whom she suspected to be her son in a Yugoslav orphanage in Belgrade. In correspondence the youth recalled a rocking horse that he had had as a child, and his description of it, and of the family home in Belgrade, convinced Mrs. Etzl that she had found her boy. When these clues and the other identification evidence were laid before his sister Maria, she exclaimed, "He's my brother. I'm positive he's my brother!" The family was reunited amid tears of joy at the International Airport in Philadelphia, a few days before Christmas.

There is something symbolically revealing in this encounter: a girl in Philadelphia discovers that a boy in a Yugoslav orphanage is her true brother. The higher meaning and symbol of that discovery is that when we see Jesus we find persons in all the haunts of wretchedness and need throughout the world who are truly our brothers. To make this discovery is to step out of an imprisoning door into a life with dimensions of great purpose. To see Jesus is to be confirmed in the enterprise of God's Kingdom, a confirmation which promises to take the emptiness out of life.

"In a raveled world, love endures." And not only endures, but is the key that would unravel the snarls and tangles that defeat us. About many people one has the impression that they are locked up within themselves, the potential power for goodness and mercy immobilized, frozen, imprisoned. If someone could only release them from themselves! In one of Lewis Carroll's fantasies a Lock ran continually hither and thither feverishly hunting for something. Someone asked, "What is the matter?" "I'm seeking," said the Lock, "for something to unlock me." This is every man's need: someone to unlock him, to release the powers of love, to set free the impulses to generosity, to open the prison door of ourselves. In Christ we find this Key, for his perfect love casts out our fears, the fears which keep us tied up within ourselves. The gift of this kind of love is the gift of God's grace. It comes by utter trust, the abandonment of self to God's upholding, the saying to God, "Lead me in thy truth, or 'troth'—in thy faithfulness." In the supporting love of God revealed to us in Jesus Christ, we have no more fear to abandon ourselves in love of our neighbor.

Third, the gospel has one more word for a raveled world: the Lord God omnipotent reigneth! This word is spoken to an ultimate meaninglessness to which life falls prey when we face the possibility of the destruction of mankind. Dr. J. Robert Oppenheimer began an article with the proviso, "It is possible that in the larger light of history, if, indeed, there is to be a history. . . ." In these words he has gathered up the whole framework against which we have now to live our lives. We would see Jesus here, because unless we see him here it matters little whether we see him anywhere else. But we do see Jesus here and he does restore life's lost meaning. Jesus said to Martha, "Whoever lives and believes in me shall never die." By this declaration he transfers the ultimate meaning of life to the dimensions of eternity. The final significance of life is not at the mercy of a bomb or any other evil design. If the long travail of man's history were merely toward a final "peace on earth," then the threat of extinction before that peace is won would unsettle the faith of the bravest. True, the present possibility of annihilation in nuclear warfare does put any faith under severe stress. But peace on earth is not the destiny and ultimate purpose to which Christ calls us. Important though this life be, central as Jesus' concern for peace on earth undoubtedly is, and however imperative his commands, when Jesus says, "I appoint unto you a kingdom," he is not talking about a refined United Nations. It is a kingdom of the spirit against which the gates of hell shall not prevail. In all truth we must recognize this as an "other-worldly" faith. But in quite an astonishing way the person who finds this new other-worldly measurement of life in Christ, far from taking flight out of this world, plunges back into it with unsuspected motivation. If life has a glory in eternity, it has a glory upon it that can be seen and felt here and now. If life is destined for eternity it becomes the object of highest dedication in the life we live in this world.

Our Christian forefathers, although they knew nothing of nuclear physics, were living in a kind of world where they faced the same threat of destruction and catastrophe that we now face. Their earthly hopes lay under the same awesome shadow as our own. They knew what it was to face annihilation. Millions of Asians have lived under the shadow of starvation for centuries and millions of them have died in indescribable famine. The Jews have faced annihilation by pogrom and persecution for at least thirty-five hundred years, if not more. The Negro knows what it is to live beneath the threatening clouds of death and terror. And what of Frankfort, Hamburg, Coventry, Stalingrad? In its deepest significance this is hardly a new age. Others before us, and others around us, have said, "If we have a history. . . ." Millions of them had no history. The new factor in the present threat is the totality of destruction. This adds dimensions that we have never faced before. But the threat of "no history" as it confronts each of us, and as it jeopardizes the communities of mankind, is the same threat men have faced always. This realization ought to save us from the helpless and hopeless belief that the world has suddenly turned the corner into a new and terrifying age, wholly outside human experience, altogether beyond the providence of God, and without ultimate meaning.

The earliest Christians did not despair in that first age so filled with sharp menace. After facing the terrifying prospects that shadowed them, they gave voice to a cry of exaltation, "The kingdom of this world has become the kingdom of our Lord and of his Christ, and he shall reign forever and ever." These Christians knew that Rome did not hold the key to history. God ruled the heavens and the earth. And those earliest followers of Christ gave stirring witness to their faith, even in Caesar's household, and in the daily face of disaster. They believed that God still had a great purpose for the world; that the kingdoms of this world would become the kingdoms of our Lord and of His Christ. They believed that God had a purpose for their lives and, like Christians in all ages, in the face of persecution and death they went patiently, quietly, trustfully about the tasks that God had given them, confident that in His own way and season, He who was able to redeem what looked like the meaningless defeat of Christ on the cross could redeem the present also.

Life Fashioned in the Style of Christ

CHRIST, THE TEACHER

"HE taught them as one who had authority." Thus does Matthew add a postscript to the Sermon on the Mount, as though to say: these words command us by their own authority; this man has need of no further warrant. This was the impression Jesus made on his disciples and on the common people. Others bear similar witness. Listen to Mary Magdalene's first word to her risen Lord, "Rabboni!" (which means Teacher). Did not the common people hear him gladly? The disciples, on one occasion when Jesus asked them if they too would draw back from him as so many others had done, answered, "Lord, to whom shall we go? You have the words of eternal life." Jesus was Teacher. Out of moral wastelands and social wilderness, out of ethical uncertainty and personal distraction, come seekers for the truth with their plea, "We would see Jesus to find a word we can believe and a rule we can trust."

A minister recently found himself within a single day five times face to face with people in whom he recognized either the need or the desire to see Jesus.

There came to his study in the morning a young couple soon to be married. The pastor talked with them about their love, their plans for a home and family, and finally about their wedding. They read over the marriage service together, pausing over the words, "No other ties are more tender, no other vows more sacred than those you now assume. If these solemn vows be kept inviolate, and if steadfastly you endeavor to do the will of your heavenly Father, your life will be full of joy and the home which you are establishing will abide in peace." To this the girl said, "We want our home to be a religious home." A religious home could be many things, but the minister read in her wistful eyes, "We would see Jesus." Her words and her needs call to remembrance older words in which Jesus spoke of marriage in its sacramental nature: "A man shall leave his father and mother and be joined to his wife, and the two shall become one. What, therefore, God has joined together. . . ." That couple needed Jesus as Teacher of their marriage.

Later that morning a man came to see his pastor, weighing a decision whether to resign his present position and seek a new venture in vocation. The conversation that ensued took account of the man's desire to be useful, to find security, to be employed at satisfying work, to apply his skills and aptitudes where they would net the most advantage to himself and the community needs. Jesus' name did not enter the conversation. But this man needed Jesus as Teacher to his vocation, for there came a question of old, "Good Teacher, what must I do to inherit eternal life?"

On the same day the minister sat at a vice-president's desk in a large city bank waiting for an appointment. Nearby, unbroken queues of people were depositing money at cashiers' windows. It would have been surprising had even the thought of Jesus crossed the mind of a single one in that line. But in his mind's eye, the minister saw another lineup, "And he sat down opposite the treasury and watched the multitudes putting money into the treasury." John adds these words, perhaps to this occasion or a similar one: "These words he spoke in the treasury." In no place is the need more imperative for Jesus' word to be spoken. Perhaps many in the treasury would rather not see Jesus. But when men dispose of the substance of the earth they need to see Jesus in sight and heart.

In the same afternoon this pastor had one more encounter with people where he and they together sought the rule of Jesus for their common life. A family was offended at Negroes coming to a "white" church. Seeking to justify their attitude, they said, "But it isn't as though they were our neighbors." And so they were not —by geographical proximity. But the minister, seeking further for the mind of Christ, asked: "Who is your neighbor?" It was a question that echoed down the long centuries.

As that day drew to its close, the minister sat with his own daughter to share her concern for her school friend, taunted and mocked by a cruel crowd. What should she do about this unpopular girl? Where should she stand? Her father knew that until his daughter and all the others could see Jesus, this ill will could not be healed.

These five—entering a marriage, a vocation, a bank, a brotherhood, a friendship—seemed like the Greek saying to Philip, "We would see Jesus as Teacher and Ruler of all the affairs of our lives." But why Jesus? What is there in him to constrain us in marriage or market place, race or nation, in the twentieth century? How is his word a lamp to our feet, a light to our path? By what authority would we pay him heed?

First of all Jesus himself had the aspect of authority. "He taught them as one having authority." There was in the very sound of his voice and the look of his eye that which compelled serious response —either opposition or commitment; his impression was authoritative. He had no credentials of study or ordination. Yet Nicodemus, a member of the Sanhedrin, confessed to him: "Rabbi, we know you are a teacher come from God." The authority of Jesus, the Teacher, is not in a code of law, or a book of teachings, but in the proclamation of good news. What we find in Jesus is not rules, but ruling considerations; not precepts, but principles; not detailed counsel, but great concern; not so much specific laws, but commanding loyalties. His teaching is by spirit, by the interpretation of the meaning of life, in the light of which we can make our choices and can find our way in the wilderness where we live.

If there is one word to sum up the impression of Jesus' authority it might be the word *style*. There is an unmistakable style in the way Jesus lived, and the Christian life has a style to it that is recognizable anywhere. It is more than a matter of keeping rules and regulations, just as playing Chopin is more than a matter of hitting the proper notes in the proper sequence on a keyboard; Chopin has a style that is Chopin! It is more than a matter of fulfilling obligations, even as the style of your family life is more than a matter of fulfilling the minimum obligations to keep your home in operation; your family life has a style that is you! In the same way the Christian life has a style that is Christian. It is the style of great loyalty, surpassing commitment, and profound confidence that sweeps all before it.

The Christian style is what makes the difference. Peter had it. He had not kept all the laws, fulfilled all the obligations. But he had the style to be a disciple. The Rich Young Ruler lacked it. He kept all the rules and regulations from his youth up. But the style of all-out commitment he did not have. What we seek in Christ, the Teacher, is a way, a design, but most of all a *style* for the good life. His authority in this is clear, for he knew the mind of God and, if you will, the style of God, as none other has ever perceived. If the decisions I make in my marriage, my vocation, my bank, my friendships can be patterned after the mind I see in Christ, and lived in his style, I trust that my life will be in closer harmony with the will and purpose which is over all life. That is why I come seeking the Teacher come from God, to fashion my life in his style.

First, the disciple who seeks the mind of Christ finds a ruling consideration all the way through: *the expenditure of life in the love of God.* This is his style. Jesus taught not the cautious conservation of life, but its extravagant expenditure. "He that would save his life shall lose it. And he that shall lose his life for my sake and the gospel's, shall find it." In other words, we are expendable for God. Jesus often teaches us through symbol and demonstration what words could not contain. Never more persuasively did he teach anything than at the Last Supper when he took the towel, knelt down, and began to wash his disciples' feet—a menial, disagreeable service, beneath the dignity of any of the twelve disciples. He said to them: "If I wash your feet, you ought to wash each other's feet." It was the symbol of the towel and the servant. If any man would be his disciple, he must take the towel. Whether it is a man in his business, a citizen in his city, America in the family of nations, this is the measurement and the style by which conduct shall be judged. He takes the towel to become the servant of all. "He who would be great among you let him be the servant of all."

This is the making of a Christian marriage, that partners will take the towel in menial service, starting perhaps with the dish towel but going on to the towel of complete self-giving. This is the mark of true Christian vocation, that life be used up in order that a better life may be known. This consideration will not direct whether a man shall work in steel, or oil, or chemicals, or law, or in a business office, or in a factory. It will dictate that somehow his energies and capacities serve the whole good of the human family. Because so many possible vocations are ambiguous, many of us find ourselves unwillingly caught in a system that brings both blessing and curse from the same labor; one must often spend himself further for God in the things to which he devotes his leisure as well as his labor. Blessed are the men and women in communities around the world who have learned from Christ to take the towel of serving: in hospitals and homes, in charities and churches, in schools and social service, and in the continuance of a job because the work is worthy! Jesus taught through demonstration; he took the towel.

Jesus' disciples also teach us by symbol. Not long ago a Hungarian, Dr. Paul Radnai, having arrived in the United States as a refugee and exile from Communism, made a modest gift on his first Christmas in the United States. The gift was one pint of blood. He said, "I have nothing else but my healthy blood to give. I would like to offer blood to anyone who needs it. I would prefer a child." Is this not the perfect symbol against which to measure all the choices and the decisions we make? Life's blood given as a gift to God! How shabby are most of our choices, how shoddy the spirit of our human relations, how dreary our style in the face of that! What is there in the offering of our days that would reflect the teaching of Jesus: "If any man would be my disciple let him take up his cross"? The cross is nothing less than the risk of life itself and all the security we guard so defensively. There is teaching of Jesus here for the girl who asked her father what was her duty in her friendship. She must weigh popularity and the inner security which it brings against mercy in friendship and the insecurity which that would bring. The answer is not spelled out in the New Testament. In the spirit of Jesus, however, we hear a command to leave everything else for his sake, even security. Inasmuch as you ministered unto the least in some prison of fear or loneliness, or need, you did it unto me. This means insecurity. But as Peter Bertocci has said, this is where the teachings of Jesus lead "to creative insecurity rather than 'peace of mind,' to blessedness rather than 'happiness,' to moral maturity rather than psychological 'integration,' to growth rather than 'rest,' to forgiveness rather than prudential 'goodness.' . . . Only a religion that would accept insecurity can destroy evil and purify life."[1]

If there is teaching for the girl who would face the demands of friendship, there is guidance here also for the industrialist and the worker who would act responsibly in labor conflict, each risking some measure of his security for growth, understanding, and peace. What comes forth will be a "peace in tension"—but this is the creative way. The Teacher promised not peace but a sword in the tribulations of this life. "In the world you shall have tribulation." The disciple is not above his Lord! It will come to us, too—but Jesus taught us this way to walk.

Second, as we sit at the feet of Jesus, the Teacher, seeking to know his mind, to pattern after his style, over and over we hear this refrain: *the stewardship of possession.* Jesus talked more about the relation of man to property than about any other subject except God. He gave more time to teaching on possessions than he did to regeneration, prayer, faith, or the future life. Sixteen of his thirty-eight parables, one verse out of every seven in the four

Gospels—in fact, one-half of his teachings—relate to the subject of money and possessions. "You cannot serve God and mammon." All that we have we hold in trust from God. The most searching examination any man ever faces before God is the judgment of what he does with his possessions. For Jesus taught that we are stewards of God's endowments, and if this is true, it make a difference in the way we handle every relationship of our lives.

I believe I need to see Jesus before I go to the treasury. In him I find the saving reminder that my money is not my own, that God is the true provider of all that I have. The Teacher told a parable of a rich fool who tore down his barns and put up bigger barns in order to store all of his goods. He spoke of *my* crops, *my* barns, *my* goods, as though these things belonged to him. One can hardly get to be a bigger fool than that. Our crops, our barns, our goods, our money do not belong to us. They belong to God, who has entrusted them to us for as long as we live, or as long as we see fit to hold on to them and use them. But they are His, and we are stewards of His bounties, responsible for their use, and everything, at the last, is returnable to God. The tragedy is that love of accumulation crowds out the love of God. As someone has wisely summed it up, devotion to God and devotion to money are incompatible loyalties. This goes to the very heart of life. Albert Edward Bailey has described it:

When the love of money takes possession of the soul, one by one the virtues leave and the vices arrive. First, the fountains of sympathy are stopped; then the pride of life looks out at the windows—one sees the "highbrow" and the "automobile face"; then arises the will to dominate rather than to serve; and last, that worst abuse of riches, when it disjoins remorse from power. Jesus knew the whole devolution of the type; and he sounded to his disciples the clearest notes of warning: "Lay not up for yourselves treasures upon the earth . . . you cannot serve God and mammon."[2]

If Jesus Christ does not become sovereign over my possessions, almost certainly I will try to make myself lord of all I possess, and it has been demonstrated that men cannot easily handle prosperity on their own.

Add to all this the problem of what we do with our wealth in a world of want. The living standards of the American people are approximately three times as high as those of European people, and somewhere between five and ten times higher than those of the people of Asia. The per capita income in the United States is now $1700. In the underdeveloped areas of the world, which include two-thirds of the earth, the average is $80. In the face of all of this, the Teacher is saying, "You had better let me direct your stewardship, for there is dangerous passage ahead."

Again in symbol the great consideration lies open to our gaze in a language beyond words. Ronald Bridges once told how he found help in carrying a small pocket cross with his coins, for no one to see but himself: "A dozen times an hour my fingers touch the cross in my pocket. The miracle of thought is such that for a small part of a second I pause, and there flashes across the tiny interval the whole drama of a great human and divine event. When I take out my money the cross is there and I am reminded again of my stewardship." Perhaps some do not need tangible reminders. Others see Jesus more easily when the symbol of divine love touches the symbols of human possessions. But the great teaching is that God must own it all.

Third, one need not seek long or far for the mind and style of the Teacher to discover this imperative concern: *that we recognize our kinship with all men in the family of God*, brothers to Christ, and to one another. The words are worn so smooth—brotherhood of man—that they slip easily out of our grasp. Could we see once again, with fresh revelation, what it means that we are brothers? William Barclay tells the story of Egerton Young, who first preached the gospel to the Indians in Saskatchewan. He found that the idea of the fatherhood of God fascinated men who had hitherto seen God only in the thunder and lightning and the storm blast. An old Chief said to Egerton Young, "Did I hear you say to God, 'Our Father'?" "I did," said Young. "God is your Father?"

asked the Chief. "Yes." "And," went on the Chief, "he is also my Father?" "He certainly is," said Young. Suddenly the Chief's face lit up with a new radiance. His hand went out. "Then, you and I are brothers," he said, like a man making a dazzling discovery. To really discover afresh that we are brothers to every other person in the family of God is a dazzling discovery for anyone to make. But from first to last the Teacher is calling us to great concern for all our brothers. It is the kind of concern exemplified by a simple servant girl with no education, who yet had a deep concern in her heart for all the family of men. Her story is told by John Henry Jowett, a great British preacher of a generation ago. When Jowett asked her how she proposed to live the Christian life, she answered, "I haven't much time left from my work, Sir, and I can't attend many meetings or even many services." Jowett then asked her, "What do you do?" She replied, "Well, Sir, I always take the daily paper to bed with me at night." Jowett was puzzled. "What's the good of that?" he asked. "Well, Sir, I look at the first page and I read the birth notices, and I pray for the babies that have been born; and I read the marriages and I pray that they may be happy and true; and I read the deaths, and I pray that God's comfort may come to these sorrowing homes." The girl was not far from the Kingdom. The brotherhood of man reaches out in the spirit of that girl to every person in his need. *Segregation* and *family* are unthinkable together. As long as we persist in broken brotherhood we have no part with Christ.

Nathaniel Micklem calls Charles Péguy, the French philosopher, poet, Socialist, who was killed in World War I, to witness for what Christ compels. Péguy lived nearly all his days unreconciled to his church, although he was profoundly Christian in heart and faith. He longed to go to Mass, but the church forbade his comrades to come, threatening them with hellfire. Therefore, Péguy would not go to Mass if they were kept away whose need was as great as his. He could not believe that one could be saved in isolation from his brethren. "We must be saved together; we must come to God together," he said. "What would God say to us if we came alone before him? Would he not say, 'Where are the others?' " It is not an American-faced Christ that we seek as a Teacher, as was sought for statuary in Hollywood's Forest Lawn Cemetery, but a Christ who wears a face of all the world, who must teach us brotherhood in the family of men.

Fourth, and paramount over all in the teachings and style of Jesus, is the persuasion that *our citizenship is in the Kingdom of God.* "The Kingdom of heaven is at hand, repent and believe the Gospel. . . . It is finished." From his first appearance in Galilee to his last word from the cross, Jesus taught and proclaimed the Kingdom of God. Any life that would be Christian in character and style must now be in the character and style of that Kingdom of heaven which has come in Jesus Christ. Jesus taught that the life which would be faithful to God would be obedient to the demands of his Kingdom. Family life, community life, economic life—these are all provinces of the Kingdom of heaven. Life in the provinces must conform to the sovereign rule of the mother country.

Happily the day of colonial rule is passing from our world. We rejoice in the freedom and independence that have come to former subject peoples. Yet we may borrow a picture from colonial days as analogy to our life here on earth. When Britain ruled India in years gone by, those who went out to live as agents of the Empire established colonies of the homeland in the midst of alien life. They observed British customs and laws, practiced British ways, even dressed for dinner, incongruous though such amenities seemed amid the primitive culture where they dwelt. Their community, their family—indeed, their lives—were constrained by the homeland in which they held citizenship.

Our dwelling is in the tents of the world. But our real citizenship as Christians is in a Kingdom not of this world. The person who is loyal to his citizenship will order his life by the standards of his Sovereign, the ways of his "home," the style of his Master. The Beatitudes describe this way. The parables of the Kingdom describe this way: the Last Judgment, the Pearl of Great Price.

In a Christian home, because we know it to be an outpost of the Kingdom of heaven, love will suffer long and be kind, love will not seek her own, love will bear all things, believe all things, hope all things, endure all things, for this is the way of our Sovereign. When Paul wrote those words to the Corinthians he was giving us perhaps the finest description of the style of Jesus Christ that anyone ever wrote. We will not violate our neighbor's integrity, for he, too, has the same Kingdom rights that we possess. To live in the provinces of the Kingdom of God is to have as life's purpose the redemption of this age, even such small corner of it as we may inhabit. But we redeem it only when we see beyond it. Someone once remarked of the French writer Bousset, "He saw all around his age, but he did not see beyond it." Jesus saw all around his age more clearly than any other, but he saw a Kingdom beyond his age, and his teaching is that his age, or any age, is redeemed only as vision and love come from beyond the age to transform it.

"Seek ye first the kingdom of God." Jesus' way is to seek it first in all the outposts, to claim these for God—homes, schools, treasuries, cities, churches. It is God's intention to give us the Kingdom in His own good time and in His own way. It is for us to be ready, seeking, and waiting. To live in the style of Christ is to live the life of surpassing commitment.

On what authority shall we take these teachings? In a sense they are self-authenticating—we find our truest fulfillment in spending ourselves for God and the Kingdom. In a sense these teachings verify themselves because *they have, and they are, their own reward*. Emerson once said of Seneca, "His thoughts are excellent if only he had the right to utter them." But the compelling authority of Jesus is in the Teacher himself. The Teacher who comes from God does have the right to his words and constrains us by his own Spirit. Arthur Gossip reminds us that Principal John Cairns once wrote to his teacher, Sir William Hamilton: "I do not know what life or lives may lie before me. But I know this, that to the end of the last of them, I shall bear your mark upon me." Those who have truly sat at the feet of

Jesus would bear the same witness, that to the end of their lives they would bear the mark of this Teacher upon themselves. We may lack precise teaching on many questions but if we bear the mark of the Master upon us we will face toward a Kingdom whose coming we seek above all other things.

VI

Our Exceeding Need and God's Exceeding Love
CHRIST, THE FORGIVING GOD

AFTER the Resurrection when Peter had returned to Galilee, disgraced and ashamed, the Lord stood one morning at the edge of the Sea of Tiberias where the disciples were fishing offshore. Learning that they had toiled all night and taken nothing, he told them to cast their nets on the other side. Presently they had more than they could haul in. Not knowing until now who it was who had spoken to them, John said to Peter, "It is the Lord." And Peter sprang into the water, thrashing his way to the feet of Jesus. Do you doubt that the reason for his wild haste was his need to be forgiven and restored to God's love? The Gospel pages are filled with records of people whose exceeding need was to be forgiven: a woman taken in adultery, a tax gatherer named Zaccheus, a Samaritan woman at a roadside well, a paralytic lying upon his couch at the feet of Jesus, a disciple turned traitor, a thief on a cross.

And our need is none other and no less than theirs. In T. S. Eliot's play *The Cocktail Party*, Edward, the discouraged husband, is pictured groping in the darkness of his own soul. Unable either to love his wife or to overcome his own self-condemnation, he describes his despair in these graphic words:

> There was a door
> And I could not open it. I could not touch the handle,
> Why could I not walk out of my prison?

. . . .

> It was only yesterday
> That damnation took place. And now I must live with it
> Day by day, hour by hour, forever and ever.[1]

This is a despair in which we may well find ourselves. More than any other place it is in the swamps and wastelands of sin that men want and need most to see Jesus.

In G. K. Chesterton's autobiography one finds an amazing confession. In explaining why he became a Roman Catholic he puts it with naked simplicity in six words. "To get rid of my sins." The same urgent need drove another man out of the Catholic Church. Martin Luther was in torment when he tried to celebrate the Mass. "I am dust and ashes and full of sin," he cried. His soul was host to all the turmoil, pang, tremor, panic, despair, desolation, and desperation which invade the spirit of man. "How can I get rid of my sin?" J. S. Whale calls this "a question that belongs to the ages." There is a tragic disharmony in life which only God's exceeding love can heal.

I remember waiting with a family one day in the halls of a hospital in a strange city to which their daughter had been brought for critical examination and possible brain surgery. A great surgeon had been called in whom they did not know. After about two hours of waiting the mother asked the nurse on the floor if Dr. Grayson had finished yet. "Dr. Grayson?" the nurse asked with some wonder. And then she said after a moment, "You must mean Dr. German. There is no one here but Dr. German who could operate on Louise."

How many times I have waited with other people in other places whose exceeding need was not brain surgery but the forgiveness of sin. They have sometimes been looking for other things, but the answer is always the same. "There is no one here but Christ who can do what you need." It is well to remember those words of C. J. Jung, coming from his experience in psychotherapy: "Apart from a person's discovery of a religious outlook on life, a vital faith, hope, and love, no one ever truly walks out of the prison of his inner failure and self-distrust and despair."

Out of this very swampland of sin, self-distrust, and despair we cry with Paul, "Wretched man that I am! Who will deliver me from this body of death?" The answer to our question is good news. "Thanks be to God through Jesus Christ!" I have heard this news and so I come saying, "I would see this Jesus who can deliver me!"

First, in my exceeding need I must *face myself as I really am*, look squarely at the truth about myself without flinching. This threatens to be so painful and costly that I will usually go to great extremes to avoid it. Were it not for God's exceeding love offered to us in Jesus Christ, would any of us have much courage to hear the truth about ourselves? Remember what Pascal said: "The knowledge of God without the knowledge of our wretchedness creates pride. The knowledge of our wretchedness without the knowledge of God creates despair. The knowledge of Jesus Christ is the middle way because in him we find both knowledge of God and of our wretchedness."

We all know how this works in the parallel matter of physical health. We begin to feel a twinge of pain somewhere inside. We try to forget it but it doesn't go away. Then we start to worry. A friend hearing of our anxiety reassures us brightly, "Oh, I had that. I think it's this muggy weather. We're all tired at this time of the year. A few days in the sun will bake it right out of you." This is the kind of reassuring news we like. With good luck our pain will all go away and we'll never have to face what's deep down inside. But after a few days in the sun the pain is still there. Able to put it off no longer we go to a doctor, who finds real trouble that neither time nor sunshine will ever cure. He discovers that we need deep and radical therapy. Could we face this knowledge about ourselves without despair unless we were in the hands of a competent physician? But merely to know that this able doctor had office hours five afternoons a week would be of no benefit to us until we went to see him and he told us the truth.

So it is with our sin. Most of us cannot face the truth about ourselves unless we are in the hands of the Great Physician. Those in whom all sensitivity is not dead feel the twinge of something wrong in their souls. Dimly they may suspect deep trouble, but such trouble is better to forget, better to avoid by cheerful pretense, better to arrest with patent nostrums, better to dismiss by basking in the light of the knowledge of God. With the character in T. S. Eliot's *Family Reunion*, "We only ask to be reassured about the noises in the cellar." But the knowledge of God that does not bring knowledge of the trouble inside ourselves creates pride. More than that, it is not really knowledge of God at all. Thank God if our pride has some weakness through which the pain of sin, the wrongness at the center of our life, still hurts!

This is the message we have heard from Jesus, that God is light, in Him is no darkness—and in His light without fear we may search the darkness within ourselves. Such darkness as this: "I have not really tried to be reconciled to those with whom I am in conflict. I have not really tried to share responsibility for *anyone* else's life." Or such darkness as this: "I could have given more to support the Christian World Mission of the Church but I do need that new car and money in the bank," even if we know that orphans are starving in Greece. Or even this greater darkness: "I have betrayed my father's hopes, I have failed my wife's trust, I have broken my children's faith, I have let my church down, and in one way or another made such a mess of my own life and the lives of others that the damage can never be repaired."

These are things no man can shuffle off by himself. A child dies in Greece whom he might have saved. A father dies with a broken heart that he might have healed. A child grows up bitter and afraid to trust because he broke his faith. If I ever come to myself in some far country and face the truth that I am a prodigal son or a prodigal husband or a prodigal father or a prodigal steward of the things that were another's, then I will cry in earnest, "Wretched man that I am, who will deliver me? I *must* see Jesus!"

Sin is self-perpetuating. Its burden increases. Consequences of our evil mount one upon another so that unless some way be found to relieve the awful weight it becomes intolerable. Some power must appear that can destroy the spreading power and poison of our sin. The fact that some people never feel the strong grip and downward pull of sin proves only that they have never faced the truth about themselves in the strong light of the Redeemer's judgment. And this is their condemnation, that light has come into the world and they love darkness rather than light.

Augustine understood what happens when evil is long continued. And he realized the radical nature of our malady.

Herein is the most just penalty of sin. That a man loses the faculty to do good when he has been unwilling to exercise it, though otherwise, had he willed it, right action would have been easy. He who against his better knowledge does not act rightly loses the knowledge of what is right; and he who has refused to do right when he could loses the power to do right when he will. For in truth, there is for every sinning soul a double penalty, loss of knowledge and loss of power.

My exceeding need is to lose my fear of the truth.

Sir Arnold Toynbee has suggested a striking metaphor in another connection that may reveal the truth here as well.

The city of Los Angeles is so large that the spectator is likely to forget that it is in reality only a tiny patch of green in a vast desert. Moreover, the grass is kept so perpetually green by constant sprinkling that it is a shock to behold the savage desert sagebrush bristling up in a vacant and untended lot. He then realizes that under the artificial green lawns the same savage nature that has here broken its way to the surface is all the time eagerly waiting for an opportunity thus to come into its own again. This is the precarious position of the intellect and the will.[2]

Is it far-fetched to think that life is like the city of Los Angeles—in this regard at least? We need someone or something that can break the spreading, choking power of sin, that can reduce and destroy the strangling hold which sin would otherwise take upon life. *In Jesus Christ we know that God has done this*. Coming into the very depths of life with a forgiving love that evil cannot provoke nor sin destroy, He destroys the spreading cancer of sin itself. When the evil exhausts itself against Him whose love out-lasts all evil, then sin is forgiven and forgotten. In the words of Charles Wesley, "He breaks the power of canceled sin."

And so it is that in God's exceeding love I can stand the truth even about myself, *because I know that it is for the saving of my life that God comes to me!* And I know that in Christ I have found a *power equal to the truth*. Painful as it may be to face it, I do not withhold anything from a doctor because the doctor will not like what he finds. The doctor's purpose is to save life. God's purpose is not to reassure me about the noises in the cellar; it is to save my soul from sin in order to further the purposes of His Kingdom. It is to go down into the cellar and overcome the demons. I am willing that He probe as deeply as need be to lay healing touch upon the cancer of sin. Moreover, I consent to His searching of my soul because it is neither desirable nor possible to hide from His understanding. It was said of Jesus, "He knew what was in man." Cried the woman of Samaria, "Come, see a man who told me all that I ever did!" Christ, the forgiving God, knows what is in us. Self-defenses are useless, hypocrisy without avail, before his gaze. Because I cannot hide what is in me, and because when God sees what is in me He loves me still, I am able at last to take my exceeding need to His exceeding love. Howard Thurman has spoken thus of love: "It is the sense of being dealt with at a point beyond all the good and beyond all the evil that is in us." When somehow through the mysteries of God's grace I know that He has met me at a point beyond all my deserving, and at a point beyond all the evil that is in me, I surrender.

Second, and for a still more urgent reason, I would see Jesus in the wasteland of sin: *my exceeding need is for God's exceeding love to release me from the prison of myself, and to bring me out of the wasteland, back home to God.* The Christian diagnosis is that we cannot release ourselves from captivity to ourselves—selves of fear, selves of greed, selves of despair. Like men locked on the inside of a prison, we cannot open the gates from the inside because we do not have the key.

For one thing, we do not have the key to release ourselves from the prison of our fears. Only One who is outside our prison, who is stronger than our fears, can do that. The writer of the First Epistle of John said: "There is no fear in love, but perfect love casts out fear." No fear in love? Do not our greatest fears come from our loves? The greater our loves, the more vulnerable we become to fright and anxiety that those we love will be hurt or destroyed. There is fear in love, but with a difference! This fear is the outreaching to another; we fear for him, for her, for them—not for ourselves. This is the suffering of love. It hurts, it consumes us, sometimes even unto death. But it is always a healing love. To be a suffering servant of another, or of a community, or of the world—this is the perfect love which casts out the unholy fear for ourselves, the nervous anxiety and distraction lest we be hurt, or eclipsed, or humbled, or obligated. In the perfect suffering love for someone else there is no fear for ourselves. The perfect love of God is the key of release from ourselves. In His love we need no longer fear anything, for nothing can destroy His love. Rather it overcomes the worst of sin and vanquishes our last enemy, death.

We do not have the key to release ourselves from the prison of pride—pride that is without humility, without forbearance, without forgiveness. With no assurance of a love to uphold us, no confidence in a love to forgive us, what help have we but to fight for position, for power, for prestige? Only One whose love seeks no position, grasps for no power, cares for no prestige, can set us free from pride.

We do not have the key to release ourselves from anxious self-concern. Only One whose love is without limits, who is outside our prison of self, can do that.

We do not have the key to release ourselves from frantic materialism. Only One who is outside the prison of our obsession with things can do that.

We do not have the key to release ourselves from despair. Only One who is outside the walls of our hopelessness, who has ven-

tured beyond the years and horizons of earth and seen the steadfast love of a heavenly Father, can do that.

But how? How can anyone—even God—do these things? Henri
Barbusse tells of a conversation overheard during the First World
War in a dugout full of wounded men. One of them knows that
he is dying and says to another: "Listen, Dominique, you've led a
bad life. There are no convictions against me. There's nothing on
the books against my name. Take my name. Take my life. I give
it to you. Straight off you've no more convictions. Take it. It's
there in my pocketbook. Go on, take it, and hand yours over to
me, so that I can carry all your crimes away with me." Said David
Roberts of these words: "At an infinitely higher level this is what
God says to the human race through Christ. 'Take my life. I give
it to you. . . . And hand your life over to me, so that I can
carry all your sins away.' "[3] When the love of God so possesses
any man's life, God's forgiveness takes away fear, pride, greed, and
despair.

No less fearful than these imprisonments is to be lost out in the
wilderness of the world, separated, estranged from God. See it
in the parallel of family relationships. Every parent sees over
again in the life of his own child what we all remember of ourselves. Few experiences put young children in such anguish as
those occasions when they feel themselves separated emotionally,
psychologically, spiritually from their parents. When this occurs
the child's exceeding need is to know himself accepted in his
parents' exceeding love, a relationship restored with father or
mother. In other words, he needs to "come home." My need is no
different before my heavenly Father. Before I lie down in safety
or face any tomorrow with assurance I must know that I am "right
with God." But how can I know unless God has shown me? No
testament would persuade me except as God Himself gives covenant. He cannot send word by someone else. It is never enough
for a neighbor or even for an older brother to assuage a child's
fears by announcement that we are all in Daddy's good graces.
Father must come. And God must come, too. In Jesus Christ we

are altogether sure that God has come. As Dr. Buttrick put it: "No longer need we say, 'If only God would walk our streets, bear our shame and say with lips like ours, Thy sins be forgiven thee.'" Cleansing has come through the God who has walked our streets and borne our shame.

Alec Vidler suggests that it is something like this:

A tradesman in a certain town found that one of his trusted men had been systematically stealing from his warehouse for years. Some people might have been soft and let him off the punishment, which is a kind of indulgence that modern men profess to admire, though they seldom practice it themselves. Other people would have been hard-boiled and would have cast the culprit adrift. But this man's employer did neither the one nor the other. He let him be tried and sentenced and sent to prison. But when the man came out of prison his employer was there to greet him with the words, "Your place is open for you. Come back. We will start afresh." And when the man reached home he found that his wages had been paid in full to his wife all the time he had been in prison. He was punished but he was forgiven. And creatively forgiven. The forgiveness of God is like that.[4]

The forgiveness of God may also be something like this: A few years ago, Greece's leper colony on bleak Spinalonga Island, off the north coast of Crete, was officially inspected after twenty years of neglect. It was condemned as a place worse than Dante's Inferno. The health ministry officials who visited the island found the 180 stricken men, women, and children living in appalling conditions, with morale so low that hatreds and jealousies were rife. But among them was one couple whose story of devotion and love moved the hearts of all who heard it. The husband had caught the disease many years ago, but his wife refused to leave him. In a gesture of supreme devotion she opened a vein in her arm and with it touched the wounds on her husband's body while he was asleep. This was twenty years ago. She was found still living with her husband. And she had never contracted leprosy! So God goes to the uttermost limit to love us in our sin and evil. So God meets us at a point beyond all the evil that we can do to Him. He stays with us and He leads us back home.

Third is the need that exceeds all my power to fill: Not only must I find the way back to God, but I *must be "right" with my brothers*. That is to say, we must be in good grace with one another. There must be a rightness about our relationship. But how can this occur unless and until I forgive them and they forgive me? And how can I do that until I myself know the forgiveness of God?

Forgiveness is a shattering experience to go through. When I come to understand the full measure of God's love for me, the enormity of what my sin has cost God, the price which He pays to love me as I am, I begin for the first time to get some measure of how much I myself have to be forgiven. Zaccheus entered somewhat into this experience. Here was a man living according to the ordinary conventional pattern of his day, certainly no saint, yet quite respectable. One day he climbed a tree to catch sight of Jesus. Was it curiosity? Was it the hope that some glimpse of the Carpenter of Nazareth would lead to good effect? We do not know. This we do know: that before Jesus had finished his visit, Zaccheus saw with new eyes the true stature of his life. He had to be forgiven fourfold. One doubts if he even knew this on the morning that Jesus came.

Likewise, how many things I learn about myself on the day when Jesus comes with judgment and forgiveness. I learn that I have been careless of responsibility. Now I see in Christ what carelessness costs in new crucifixions of justice. I see my need to be forgiven as I never saw it before. I learn that I have wasted the gifts that were given me. Now I see the high price of such waste in new crucifixions of love. I feel a strange new need to be forgiven that I never felt before. Mine may have been a coldness of heart and a wandering of mind when Jesus was on trial in my own presence. Now I see it in suffering that I should have cared about. I never knew how much I had to be forgiven!

There now remains one step more, a step I could not first

have taken but now I am able. Part of my exceeding need is to forgive those who trespass against me and to remember their sin no more. But who is sufficient for these things without God's forgiving love? Forgiveness is so costly! Its price is the giving of self to another at a point beyond all the good that is in him and beyond all the evil. It exposes one to the danger of rejection and destruction. As Howard Thurman says, "Only the experience of the love of God can perform this miracle." Outside the love of God I could not let myself go in forgiving love; I would be afraid of destroying myself. But when I see that God has forgiven me—even such a person as in His judgment I know myself to be—then have I some measure of the grace needed to forgive him who sins against me. Only in such forgiveness and reconciliation can the city of men closer approximate the City of God.

Toward the end of Graham Greene's novel *The End of the Affair*, a man makes this prayer of desperation: "Let me forget me." To this kind of prayer forgiveness is bound to lead. A prayer for the dethronement of self from life's center and the enthronement of God. Nowhere has this tension and struggle between wretchedness and assurance been more piercingly uttered than in John Donne's poem:

> Wilt thou forgive that sin where I begun,
>   Which was my sin, though it were done before?
> Wilt thou forgive that sin, through which I run
>   And do run still, though still I do deplore?
> When thou hast done, thou hast not done;
>   For I have more.
>
> Wilt thou forgive that sin, which I have won
>   Others to sin, and made my sins their door?
> Wilt thou forgive that sin, which I did shun
>   A year or two, but wallowed in a score?
> When thou hast done, thou hast not done;
>   For I have more.

I have a sin of fear, that when I've spun
    My last thread, I shall perish on the shore;
But swear by thyself, that at my death thy Son
    Shall shine, as he shines now and heretofore:
And having done that, thou hast done;
    I fear no more.

Conversation with God in His Own Tongue

CHRIST, OUR PARTNER IN PRAYER

ONE day, when Jesus had finished praying in a certain place, one of his disciples said to him, "Lord, teach us to pray." If we may judge from the Gospel record, this is the only thing the disciples ever asked Jesus specifically to teach them. This the disciples wanted more than anything else to learn. Above every other necessity they felt their need to talk with God. Was not Philip in the upper room asking the same thing when he said, "Lord, show us the Father and we shall be satisfied"? From the disciples in Galilee and Philip in the upper room to men and women in the crowded ways of twentieth-century life, Christian followers have come seeking Jesus—"Lord, teach us to pray . . . show us the Father." A little girl, while learning to pray one night, said to her father, "But Daddy, how do we know God hears us when we talk to Him? Does He ever answer us?" She asks a question out of childish curiosity that others have asked in deepest need. Burdened by an unbearable sense of guilt, desperate over his imagined failure toward his family, his employer, his church, a young man was coming regularly to his minister for help and counsel. After many weeks he exclaimed in uncontrolled anguish, "If I could only pray! Can you help me? Most of the time it seems like I'm talking to myself. I don't even know if God hears me." Lord, teach us to pray!

What can we say, how can we say it, to be sure that our prayer gets through to God? How can we know what God may say to us?

These things above all we would learn from Jesus. And we come to Jesus for the answer because he, more than any other, so lived with our heavenly Father that he can teach us the language of God's own heart. How could we put it better than a six-year-old explaining some of her theological difficulties? "I'll know Jesus," she said, "because I have seen his picture lots of times. But I won't know God because I've never seen His picture." Then after a moment she went on brightly, "But that will be all right. Jesus will introduce me to God." It is one of the supreme ministries of Jesus that he does introduce us to God. "He that has seen me has seen the Father." Jesus does teach us to talk with God in God's own tongue, "When you pray say . . ."

There is a language of prayer. But let us be fairly warned: prayer is no pleasant formula for peace of mind. Prayer can overwhelm us, shaking life to its innermost depths of mind and soul, leaving nothing unchanged. Men of ancient Israel were aware of the consequences of coming face to face with God. They may have been wrong in their belief that he who looked upon God would die, but their instinct was true. If a person has really talked with God in His own tongue, his life will not be the same at the close of prayer. Even so, "Lord, teach us to pray."

First, prayer's tongue includes the *language of love between Father and son*. No matter what my need, this is where conversation with God ought to begin. That I can speak to God as a son to his father, that He listens to my voice as a father to his son— this is the astounding truth about prayer towering above everything else that prayer may mean. Who am I that the Lord, the Almighty, the King of creation should turn His ear to my speaking! Yet this is the assurance of Jesus. "If you then, who are evil, know how to give good gifts to your children, how much more will your Father who is in heaven give good things to those who ask Him? . . . But when you pray, go into your room and shut the door and pray to your Father who is in secret; and your Father who sees in secret will reward you." God is a Father, and we talk to Him as a son to his father.

Every man who is a father has heard the call "Daddy" a hundred times a day. His child's interests may range from momentary whims to troubled concern. But more important than any of these is the fact that the child can call and the father will answer. Greater by far than the details of any conversation a father has with his child is the fact that they can talk together. Jesus knew this kind of relationship with God, and he tells us we can know God in the same way. At the heart of creation is One whom we may call Father, One who calls us son. This is a language so many of the hopeless would come to Jesus to learn if they knew he could teach them. For this legion of forlorn human derelicts Stephen Vincent Benét has written what he calls a "Minor Litany":

> This being a time confused and with a few clear stars
> Either private or public
> Out of its darkness I make a litany
> For the lost, for the half-lost, for the desperate:
> Chloral have mercy on us
> Luminal have mercy on us
> Nembutal have mercy on us
> Freud have mercy on us
> Life have mercy on us.[1]

Jesus teaches us to say, "Father have mercy on us."

One of the most vivid pictures in modern poetry is the strange figure in Walter de la Mare's "The Listeners":

> "Is there anybody there?" said the Traveler,
>   Knocking on the moonlit door;
> ....
> And he smote upon the door again a second time;
>   "Is there anybody there?" he said.
> But no one descended to the Traveler;
>   No head from the leaf-fringed sill
> Leaned over and looked into his gray eyes,
>   Where he stood perplexed and still.[2]

Whatever the poet may have intended by these lines, surely this could be the image of us all in some experience with prayer, saying in doubt, "Is there anybody there?" Standing on the sill of some sorrow, before the door of some imperious demand, we knock and ask, "Is there anybody there?" And only silence comes back, not even a head to look over into our eyes. Such praying is the experience sometimes even of the saints. But Christian assurance promises that our Father waits behind every door of petition, answers every knock of supplication, looks from above with tenderness upon every intercession. "Your heavenly Father knows that you need all these things. . . . The Holy Spirit, whom the Father will send in my name, will abide with you forever." Taking Jesus at his word, we may with confidence draw near to the throne of grace. It is to Him who sits upon that throne that we may talk, for He is our Father.

If we may talk to God in this language of son to father, if in this same tongue He speaks to us as Father to son, two transforming consequences follow. One is the *coming of strength*, the other is *self-acceptance*. An old story is told of a man who was asked if he had found any shade in crossing the desert. He said he had found shade but he couldn't get into it. When queried as to why not, he replied, "Have you ever tried to sit down in your own shadow?" A life without prayer is like nothing more than trying to sit down in our own shadow. Under burning sun, traveling across parched wasteland affording no oasis against either heat or thirst, we try to take refuge in the shadow of ourselves. But a man overcome by guilt, a woman appalled by her own insufficiency, a youth alarmed at life's demands find their own shadows no refuge. Then comes the Master to give us a strength not our own, to lead us to a sanctuary above ourselves. "He who dwells in the shelter of the Most High, who abides in the shadow of the Almighty, will say to the Lord, 'My refuge and my fortress; my God, in whom I trust.' " There is a strength in the sheltering love of a Father who loves His children, a strength these children take with them even when they go forth to cross the sands of fiercest duty and untempered discipline. To know that they may speak to God who hears them when they call steadies them at noonday and shelters them by night. Ellen Glasgow describes this assurance and the consequences as they came to one of her characters in *Vein of Iron:*

While the old woman sat there a sudden vertigo rushed over her—as if every object in the room had become menacing and alive. To save herself from falling out of her chair she clutched the edge of the table, startled, astonished, incredulous. In front of her yawned a bottomless pit, outside and beyond the infinite mercy. Then, just as the room and the earth were about to give way under her feet, she said aloud, "The Lord has never failed me, I am in the hands of the Lord." While the chant pealed through her mind equilibrium was restored, faith balanced itself on its throne, a fresh infusion of energy surged through her veins, and her withered heart put on greenness. For she had spoken only the truth. The Lord had never failed her. She was in the hands of the Lord.[3]

The other effect of such language of love between Father and son is *self-acceptance.* No finer gift can any parent give a child than this—that he accept himself as being loved, and forgiven. Robert Frost spoke once of home as being the place where they have to take you in when you haven't anywhere else to go. That puts it in the negative light of duty. The other side of the truth is that home can be the place where you needn't pretend to be what you are not, where you are loved for what you are, and in that love, by God's grace, transformed to what you may be. A man obsessed by guilt may be released through a father's love that steadfastly comes on and will not be turned back by sin. The man can arise from his knees to stand erect. A woman caught in the mire of frustration and failure can stand up out of the quicksand, accepting herself in all her weakness for what she is, having found on her knees that faithfulness, integrity, and love are the offerings more pleasing to God than accomplishment and success. Self-acceptance. This is the issue of love between father and son.

Now if this is the first and finest relationship of prayer, then the first duty of prayer is a quietness before God. "In quietness and confidence shall be your strength." Much prayer begins in the wrong mood; it is conversation wrongly initiated. Professor William Adams Brown once chided us for our noisy chatter when our need is for receptive meditation: "For one among us who, with Isaiah, says, 'Speak, Lord, for thy servant heareth,' there are a thousand saying, 'Listen, Lord, for thy servant speaketh.'" To some of us comes no harder discipline than this: to let God alone while we sit or kneel before Him. So says Richard Cecil: "The life of a Christian is a life of paradoxes. He must lay hold on God: he must follow hard after Him: he must determine not to let Him go. And yet he must learn to let God alone. Quietness before God is one of the most difficult of all Christian graces." But to be quiet before God will transpose even our most clamorous wants into a higher key.

Second, the vocabulary of prayer includes *the language of obedience between Master and disciple.* A young lawyer once asked Jesus in eager hopefulness, "What shall I do that I may inherit eternal life?" Nicodemus came to ask, "How can a man be born when he is old?" Was it not Peter himself who confessed to Jesus, "To whom shall we go? You have the words of eternal life." Thus, during his earthly ministry, men came to Jesus to find God's will. They come to him still. Lord, teach us to pray. But is there any speech in which we may talk to God and He to us, through which language we may learn to know His will? Jesus assumed such a tongue; numbers of followers after him have been sure now and then that they heard it. Some of us persist in the conviction that Jesus can teach it to us. Where does he begin?

He begins with us where he began with himself. He put himself utterly in God's hands. From start to finish his life of prayer began, continued, and ended as the Master abandoned himself to God. In the desert of temptation he yielded all that he had and all that he was to become to the Lord: "You shall worship the Lord your God and him only shall you serve." Persuaded of this, Jesus said, "Get thee behind me, Satan." Throughout the Galilean ministry he affirmed over and over: "My food is to do the will of Him who sent me. . . . I must go on my way. . . . It cannot be that a prophet should perish away from Jerusalem." In the darkest anguish of his passion he prayed the same, "Not my will but thine be done." The first word in disciple's language is *surrender*. We want to do things our way; we want to keep control; we want to be master in our own house. There are three persistent reasons why this language comes hard to most of us. First, we may try to coerce God to bend His will to do things our way. A well-known minister speaks of prayer as a "pipeline to power." Although he goes on to admit, "Prayer is not a jackpot machine into which you drop a wishful thought, the boon you desire forthwith falling into your lap," the conclusion easily drawn from the petroleum metaphor is that prayer is essentially a way of tapping into God's limitless reserves of energy, supplying ourselves with capacity to accomplish whatever may be needed or wanted. Prayer may indeed bring strength of soul, courage, all kinds of moral capacity, but essentially prayer is not a pipeline to anything. It is a surrender to God. We are not harnessing the power of God to further any ambitions of our own; we are asking God to take over our own ambitions.

Again, this language comes hard because, whether consciously or not, much of the time we prefer our religion without God, which, as a wise observer has noted, is like steering your craft by the lights of your own masthead. There came in the mail not long ago an advertisement that seems the epitome of contemporary man's confidence. This letter was promoting a new book called *Auto-conditioning: The New Way to a Successful Life in Business.* The blurb read in part, "A marvelous power to win more profit is waiting in your mind that never sleeps. . . . Your own MIND THAT NEVER SLEEPS can help you overcome fear, frustration, doubt, and failure! It can open a treasure chest of straight-thinking ability, selling talent, confidence and organizing strength! . . . Successful men and women direct themselves from within. It is almost as though they speak to a magic genie inside them who delivered to these fortunate people whatever they wanted out of life." Even those who would be less shameless in proclaiming their own automatic power to achieve "success" try, nevertheless, to steer their course from lights on their own mast. "My political prejudice is the right way to proceed. I will steer my course from its light. Lord, help me to follow my light." "My philosophy of money is the only sensible one. Lord, help me to keep my budget." "My business methods are best. Lord, help me to reach my quotas and my goals." So we resist surrender, steadfastly refusing to look above the masthead to the stars.

Most subtle of all is a third difficulty. We do not want even to be served by God. We cannot relinquish pride even long enough to step down and let God do for us; rather we must do for Him. Peter loudly protested that Jesus could not wash his feet. He would wash the Master's feet. Prayer comes especially hard to the faithful disciple who, out of devoted consecration, so insists on doing for God what he will not let God do for him.

In what vocabulary will we hear God speaking when He answers our prayers as Master to disciple? If we understand four words we shall know enough to understand Him.

1. "He who loses his life for my sake shall find it. . . . Take up your cross and follow me." Of any choice you make, one question will come first: Do I lose my life in this for Christ's sake? In other words, does Christ lay claim to my first allegiance; are my strength and purpose committed to him in this regard? Am I putting my own ambition in the service of his purposes, or does my satisfaction come first?

2. "You cannot serve God and mammon. . . . Seek first the kingdom of God." In all choices we must check ourselves with the question: Do my possessions rule my life? Am I beholden to personal security above the consideration of God's Kingdom? Am I a slave of mammon or do I know the glorious liberty of the children of God because I am captive to a Kingdom that promises no security but the joy of obedience?

3. "Inasmuch as you have done it unto the least of these, my brethren, you have done it unto me." What will be the results of my choices in all things? Will they minister to a larger life for the

children of God affected by my behavior? Will someone have a harder time on my account? Do I close doors through which others might pass to more abundant life?

4. "Go ye into all the world teaching them." Will what I contemplate doing teach any man the good news of God? Where is the witness in what I do? Will it persuade others, will it discourage any? Paul wrote to the Galatians, "Because of me they glorified God." If this were to be the epitaph of my life I could ask for no more.

These are God's words—*cross, kingdom, serving, witness*. If we are still, knowing that it God's time for speaking, not ours; if we look above the mast to the stars, we will hear these words and perhaps know His will.

Some time ago two disasters shocked the world: the sinking of the *Andrea Doria* and the collision of two airliners high above the Grand Canyon. Both occurred in the fog and in each case there were within the planes and ships instruments to prevent the disasters. Radar enables men to "see in the dark," permitting a pilot to keep his course clear of all obstacles. These incidents offer striking parallel to our spiritual situation. If every day we will fix our course on God, allow His presence to be felt, if every day we will hear His words of direction, cross, kingdom, serving, and witness, we may keep clear of collisions that would bring life to disaster. Rarely will specific instructions come to us in prayer. Stories of such are exciting to read—how a book fell open to show guidance on some printed page, audible voices speaking, and all the rest. What we do gain are directions, perspectives, awareness of dangers which we heretofore had not noticed. Most of all, we gain a sense of walking with One who will be responsible with us in the outcome. The person who has really felt the presence of God, who has made a decision according to what he understood to be God's will, will be able to say with a clear conscience, "God and I were together when this was done and we will be together whatever may come from it."

Third, the tongue in which prayer is spoken is *the language of mercy between giver and intercessor.* The Psalmist tells us that the mercy of the Lord is from everlasting to everlasting. The author of the Letter to the Hebrews spelled out in words what people who met Jesus firsthand ascertained for themselves—he ever lived to make intercession for us. The consequence has been that men, women, and children throughout the Christian age have come to Jesus in hope that if they prayed through him God might answer their supplications.

Suppose that while a great surgeon was speaking to a crowded assembly in New York, some men mounted to the roof, smashed a hole in the ceiling, and, before they could be restrained, lowered a cripple by stretcher to the feet of the doctor? Such frantic resort might be more devoted than wise, but it would leave no question that these men were desperate in their desire to bring their patient to healing hands. This happened once in the presence of Jesus. Hardly a page of the Gospel passes but we read how someone in frenzied hopefulness was brought to Jesus for healing.

Time does not change. We no longer seek the touch of Jesus' hand for our brothers' needs, but the presence of God's love through Christ remains real and undiminished in His healing of our souls. Our prayers must be no less extreme than knocking a hole through the roof. Prayer has no holier purpose than to bring others to God. On what basis do we consider that this appeal for mercy—the language of supplication between intercessor and giver —is an appropriate tongue in which to pray? For one thing, Jesus did it. In his high-priestly prayer spoken in the presence of the disciples in the upper room, Jesus prayed for his followers and for all who would believe through them. If intercession were not a language pleasing to God, would Jesus have used it? Moreover, Jesus promised, "Ask whatever you will in my name and I will do it"—a promise more often impossible to believe than otherwise; nevertheless, the assurance of Jesus, to be taken on faith. And if we do take it on faith, surely we cannot suppose that God would answer every kind of prayer except the fondest supplications of love. Above all, Jesus in no wise ever cast anyone out who was brought to him for mercy and healing. If indeed he and the Father were one, and are one still, then could we suppose that God cares less for our intercessions than did Jesus? Or that He lacks the means by which the gifts of mercy and healing can be given? "Pray for me," says a friend facing some towering need. "Without your prayers I shall fail." Why? Does God not care what happens? Does He depend on us for what He alone cannot do? Augustine once wrote, "Without God we cannot; without us God will not." It was a way of saying two things: We depend on God, God depends on us. This does not limit what God might do; it does not restrain His love. But God is to us as a father to his family of children. Notwithstanding his boundless love toward them, he yet needs their love toward one another.

Of course, there is one sense in which all this is idle talk. Whatever our reasoned theology, we do pray for those we love.

> When hearts are full of yearning tenderness
> For the loved absent, whom we cannot reach
> By deed or token, gesture or kind speech,
> The spirit's true affection to express;—
> When hearts are full of innermost distress,
> And we are doomed to stand inactive by,
> Watching the soul's or body's agony,
> Which human effort helps not to make less—
> Then like a cup capacious to contain
> The overflowings of the heart is prayer:
> The longing of the soul is satisfied,
> The keenest darts of anguish blunted are;
> And though we cannot cease to yearn or grieve,
> Yet we have learned in patience to abide.[4]

If nothing else (and here even the agnostic would agree), intercession at least bestows this not inconsiderable blessing on the one who intercedes.

Beyond that, when we have prayed for others we ourselves become better instruments of God's love. It is impossible to harbor animosity toward one for whom we constantly intercede before

God. We are not as prone to forget the cry of need from any for whom we have prayed. Wise students of human behavior have called tenderness the indispensable emotion. Our feelings are not necessarily tender because we have prayed for God's mercy on others. But hardly can anyone be tender without such asking.

But these are all secondary effects, in a sense selfish concomitants of intercession. What of the direct consequences? Most important of all, prayers of intercession create an unbroken channel for the mingling of our own love with God's power and love. As we reach out in love toward some remembered person, reaching out at the same time in supplication to God, the way is prepared for spiritual strength to go from us to them through God's intercession. We do stand here on the edge of great mystery. But at the heart of this mystery we see Jesus. He prayed for those he loved. He prayed for us. And he told us to pray for each other.

And yet we must ever abide the terrible tension between God's promises and His silence. We pray because we have God's promise of faithfulness: "Whatever you ask in my name I will do it that the Father may be glorified in the Son." Nevertheless, one day a number of years ago I met a colleague of mine in the children's ward of the New Haven Hospital. Inquiring for his health and news of his family, I learned that his little boy was a patient there, suffering from leukemia. Knowing the pride and joy and love which this young lad had brought to his father and how much anticipation he had for their life together, I sensed something of the stark fear and awful anxiety that must now have filled my friend's heart and mind. In my prayers that day I poured out my heart to God. I lifted little David's life up before God, asking His mercy and protection. Thinking of all that this life could become, the good that he might do in the world, the joy that he might bring, I appealed for God's strength that this life might be spared. The next time I visited the hospital I told the father that I had prayed for his son. I wanted him to know of this surrounding love. He thanked me and told me that his congregation had held a special service of intercession for David's life. We were aware of

God's presence as we stood in that room. Three days later a friend called me to say that David had died that morning.

What shall we say to these things? We might say, first of all, that leukemia does not respond to intercessory prayer. We might also say that neither I nor the congregation, nor even David's father, knew well enough how to pray for his healing. We might say that God had another design for this boy's life that was not known to us. All of these things may be more or less true. Yet, when every explanation has been made, the tension remains between God's promises and His silence. There is more to this mystery than can be explained.

Here we must take the leap of faith. We do not know—we cannot see—but we believe! We believe that God hears, that God loves, and that our love is not wasted. We believe that God turns no deaf ear to such prayer as this:

"God, you know how we love this child because You love him even more than we do. You know what his life is worth more than we know it because You created him.

"Father, if it be possible, give him strength, give him health to live. Help us to help him in every way we can. Do Thou help him in all the ways that we cannot. Keep him in Your love, keep us in Your love. Let nothing separate us from Your love. We pray through Jesus Christ our Lord."

When a person has truly prayed like that, he sees in his prayer not primarily what he asks of God, but rather what God asks of him, that he may use every experience to do God's will and that he may commit his life and the life of those he loves into God's keeping. To pray thus is to discover with Arthur Gossip that in and through the awful tension of our prayers we have all the resources of Jesus Christ, all the grace and power from the Lord God Almighty and All-merciful, and that unless these can fail or run dry, we are well able, if we draw upon them, to do anything and everything that God may ask of us.

This is the language of prayer. On our part the petitions of a son to his Father, on His part the promises of a Father to His son. On our part the desires of the disciple toward the Master, on His part the demands of the Master upon His disciple. On our part the supplications of an intercessor, on His part the everlasting mercy of the Giver of all good things.

For Life Dispersed on Ribbon Roads

CHRIST, THE MASTER IN A COMMUNITY OF FAITH

NEAR the beginning of Jesus' ministry, and again near the end, we come upon an incident of a lonely man wanting to call Jesus Master in a community of faith. In these two men we see ourselves reflected and our same need to belong to God in a company of believers who belong to one another.

On a hillside across the Sea of Galilee there lived a man with an unclean spirit, whose dwelling was among the tombs. No longer could he be kept chained in his own home and he was driven forth to live a wild, distraught, hermit existence. Night and day, among the tombs and on the mountains he cried out, bruising himself with stones. Jesus came to this man and drove the evil, unclean spirits out of his mind. The Bible tells us they entered into a herd of swine. Then the man turned to Jesus and begged the Master that he might go with him. In some ways that is one of the most poignant and touching episodes in the Gospel. An outcast, no community to belong to, no family to include him, bruised in body and soul, he begged Jesus to let him go with him. At last he had found in Jesus healing for his illness; he wanted to go with Jesus as well to find healing for his loneliness, strength for his spirit, believing in and belonging to a beloved community where Jesus was Master.

At the other end of the Gospel came another man to Jesus with the same desire. At the very brink of death the penitent thief, crucified alongside Christ, turned and beseeched Jesus, "Remember me when you come into your kingdom." It is doubtful if this man had ever seen Jesus before. What he saw in him here in these closing hours we are not sure. But there was something in Jesus that prompted this man to call him Master. Undoubtedly his was a plea for remembrance and for forgiveness. But hardly less was it a wish to belong to the community of which Jesus was King. "When you come into your kingdom, let me come too." This man was among the first to want to see Jesus in order that he might belong to the community where Christ was Master.

And what about ourselves? In 1926 Franz Kafka wrote an allegory called *The Castle*, whose truth has become appallingly clear with the years. It is the story of a Mr. K who comes to a village to be a land surveyor for the count who lives in a great castle. But try as he may, K can never seem to reach the castle. It always recedes before his approach. While waiting, hoping and trying to enter the castle, K undertakes to settle in the village where he finds himself and become part of that community. But he somehow finds this impossible too. No one understands him; no one accepts him with confidence. He cannot relate his life to any other life. He is separate, alone, isolated from everyone. Both the castle (symbol of purpose) and the village (symbol of community) remain beyond the seeker's entrance. As Robert Nisbet recognized:

The plight of Kafka's hero is the plight of many persons in the living world: isolation, estrangement, and the compulsive search for fortresses of certainty and the equities of judgment. . . . The modern release of the individual from traditional ties of class, religion, and kinship has made him free. But his freedom is accompanied not by the sense of creative release, but by the sense of disenchantment and alienation. The alienation of man from historic moral certitudes has been followed by the sense of man's alienation from fellow man.[1]

There, but for the grace of God, do we all stand, alienated from God and separated from one another. From these shadows of alienation and aloneness come people seeking a community of love where One is loved who, from the heart of the universe, has first loved us and in whose love we find meaning and purpose.

First, there are those who come seeking a community of love in which Jesus is Master because *their lives are incomplete in lonely independence*. T. S. Eliot, in one of his Choruses from *The Rock*, points us to the heart of our condition:

> And now you live dispersed on ribbon roads
> And no man knows or cares who is his neighbor
> Unless his neighbor makes too much disturbance
> But all dash to and fro in motor cars
> Familiar with the roads and settled nowhere.[2]

It is one of the terrifying facts of our time that the centrifugal force of modern living continually whirls community all to pieces. Is there any gospel for life dispersed on ribbon roads? We would see Jesus. Perhaps more than any other the superhighway can be seen as the symbol of our life's lack of community. In city after city across America whole communities have been leveled to the ground in order to make way for superhighways. Sometimes this has had a most salutary effect in the demolition of slums. But in its symbolic dimensions it suggests that the highway may be replacing the community as the true location of our lives. These frightening words come from the pen of a Southern African looking at California's *El camino real*:

I am writing this some thirty miles away from San Francisco in a town attached to the road. In this case the town seems to be no-man's-land, not the road. Except for a house to live in, that road along its length is able to provide you with any material thing you might ever need. There are banks, travel agencies, money lenders; real estate agents who will sell you a house, and furniture stores that will sell you the furniture to fill it with; there are bookstores and shops selling the latest selection of records; there are elegant little establishments that offer you tropical fish in bowls; there are at least three or four hospitals for dogs. But the curious and frightening thing is that no one lives on the road; all these shops and facilities belong only to the road and to no city. Nowhere along its length does the road contract, confine itself, center itself for a community around it. There are no parks, no plaques commemorating notable events; there are no vistas, no views, no streets that radiate from this point or that; no steps leading to public buildings. The road runs, with all its business, from San Francisco to here and beyond, and it is as if some kind of vital tendon had been severed so that it can grasp nothing to itself, can enclose nothing in itself, can make no order of itself, but can only lie sprawling, incoherent, centerless, viewless, shapeless, faceless, offering all the products a community can need and yet making the establishment of a community impossible.[3]

We are a people on the move, who often gather in vast crowds—having no true community. Look at the people who suffer for lack of any such community and whose exceeding need is to find a company whose mark is kindness and concern. Amos Wilder suggests some of them to us:

There are countless members of broken homes, partners and children who have suffered corrosion of heart and starvation of affection. There are the victims of special psychological disasters which our modern urban Vanity Fair prepares for so many. There are the specially sensitive and gifted people, including artists and intellectuals, who have not been able to stand the impersonal Waste Lands of our dehumanized culture and who have cracked up. There are the marginal groups in business life or labor or farming on whom recurrent insecurity and false values have finally left their mark. And there are the vast number of secularized men and women who have just reached the point of meaninglessness and hollowness.[4]

All these and many more are in the throngs which pass us on the street, the parkway, the thruway. It is this "lonely crowd" who want life to be managed and directed by others, because they cannot bear the loneliness of themselves. They find no gospel in themselves, nor yet in the directed life of organization man.

Could there be some true community around Jesus Christ where I could belong to my fellows, and they to me, and we to him? Is

there some place where men and women care for one another, are
kind to one another, because they belong to one another and because they are children of God? What these people seek is here
within these walls, in the heart of this company, around the Lord's
Table. This is what with all their heart they would find, though
they call it not by name nor recognize where it is. This is what
Christ gives—a community of faith where men and women are
members one of another, where men and women can be accepted
for what they are and for who they are, where no barriers are ever
raised to keep a man or woman out. We would see Jesus in the
community of faith because we surmise we shall never be whole
ourselves until we've found "the rest of ourselves" in Christ's
household.

In Christ we find that life has a deeper meaning in the fellowship of the spirit, that life is a belonging to others that has its
basis in something more profound than language, more inclusive
than race, more commanding than nationality, stronger than creed.
Some time ago I came into the church auditorium with two new
friends who had come to us from Hungary. We could not understand a word of each other's language. The two young men, having
been through experiences that we cannot imagine, were still frightened, withdrawn within themselves, not yet entirely sure what they
might find around the next corner. But as they came through the
door and looked above the communion table, the older man took
the younger by the shoulder and pointed to the cross. A light came
on his face and a great smile broke from his lips, and he looked
at me and indicated the cross. I nodded to him with a smile, trying
to tell him by my expression that I understood. There was between
us a communion deeper than any language, for the cross has a
language of its own. In that moment we discovered that we stood
not apart from one another in lonely isolation. We were members
one of another. In that moment our lives had found more of their
meaning, they were more nearly whole. The moment was an earnest of a greater communion and community gathered into Christ.

Two reports coming from widely separated sources bear striking witness to our need to belong, our need to be needed in a community of life. In a report of the American Friends Committee, Rufus Jones commented on a five-year-old orphan who, bombed out of his home and evacuated to the country, said, "Now I'm nobody's nothing." Added Jones, concerning the war refugees, "It is very much worthwhile to help these 'nobody's nothings' to discover that somebody cares, and that somebody with a face and heart comes to save them from hopelessness and despair."

The other report comes from Bertram Beck, of the Children's Bureau, United States Department of Health, Education and Welfare, who had this to say in discussing juvenile delinquency:

It is lack of unity, of faith, of sense of purpose—this lack of feeling of *we-ness*—which lies at the root of our whole problem. . . . [But] there are parents who are so fortunate in their own personalities that despite the storms of neighborhood, community and world, they can give to their children a basic, ineradicable *sense of belonging*, one which inoculates them against the ravages of destructive economic and social forces. (It was the children of such parents who during World War II were best able to withstand the frustrations of Army life; those who cracked up under the same privations were almost always young men who "felt themselves a part of Nothing"—young men with no real sense of purpose.) [5]

Almost the same words: "part of Nothing," "nobody's nothing." Homes and churches alone cannot turn the tide of delinquency from us. But against this lostness, this lack of belonging, this lonely independence that destroys people, the company of Christian disciples can offer to men and women a *sense of belonging*, and with it a stature that comes from being needed. How are we needed in the community of faith? We are needed to "bear one another's burdens" and so fulfill the law of the Master; to put a supporting hand beneath someone's arm, to "strengthen the weak hands and make firm the feeble knees" when the way is hard; to speak an encouraging word in the dark days; to rejoice with those who rejoice, to weep with those who weep.

We are needed to bear witness in the community of faith. Someone will be watching to see whether we witness to faith or to fear, to loyalty or to lassitude. Someone may fall if we are not there to stand; someone may turn back if we are not there to go forward. The story is told of a man who had lived for many years as a Christian among non-Christian people in Asia, and who returned many seasons later to his friends in that community. He learned that during his absence the child of one of the Asians had died. The father of the child said to the Christian: "When we buried the little child I said the name of God and your name. I hope you don't mind." This is the power of witness, that in some moment of great need a person finds strength in the sound of another's name, in the recollection of testimony seen in his life. In a community where each one is loved for his own sake, and over which God keeps a tender watch that no witness be lost, no person's life or love is ever unneeded. Whether anyone else is watching or not, God watches.

We are needed in the community of faith when the congregation of believers assembles to lift up hands and hearts in holy praise. In the community of Christ we are needed.

Second, what of those who come seeking Jesus as Master in a community of faith because they want somewhere *to commit their lives to God's Kingdom?* They seek the Church in hope that here they will be commissioned in the service of that Kingdom, that here they will find release from being what Irwin Edman once called "prisoners of the moment." They want release from "the moment" by entering the age-long unbroken communion of saints who march beneath the colors of Christ in the service of God. Tired of being uncommitted, they want to stand with the prophets, disciples, martyrs, saints, reformers, and dedicated followers in all times and places. The Church is the fellowship of those who have taken up the tasks of God's Kingdom in ages past, are engaged in them in this present moment, and will shoulder them in years to come. As soon as we put our hands to the responsibilities of the Kingdom of God there comes a new measure of power. This power is from God, through the company who have found something for which they would lay down their lives, a company concerned so to live as to release the best life that is in others.

He who is held prisoner of the moment shall lose his life. He who loses his life for God's sake beyond the moment shall find his life. How much of our activity and energy and devotion goes to what is immediately expedient, to things which have no more than a fleeting importance! In his history of the Civil War, *This Hallowed Ground*, Bruce Catton says of Lee's army approaching Gettysburg: "It was on its own in a strange land, scooping up supplies from the fat Pennsylvania farming country, driven by an inexorable compulsion—lacking a supply line, it must eternally keep moving because if it did not it would starve, and whenever it found its enemy it must strike without delay no matter how the odds might look." That could be the almost perfect picture of the way great multitudes live their lives. Lacking a supply line to any great communion beyond themselves, they keep eternally moving on their own, compelled by the expediency of every passing hour, living entirely off whatever resources they find in the measure of each moment, trying, as Odell Sheppard said, to live with their roots in mid-air. After a while people want to get their roots into the soil of the centuries, they want to get out of the prison house of the moment, they become suffocated with trivial affairs, fed up with the futility of just plain business, saying, "I would see Jesus. I would be doing the King's business. I would belong to the Christian army with its great traditions of the ages. Here we find no continuing city." But in the words of Masefield,

Friends and loves have we none, nor wealth nor blest abode,
But the hope of the City of God at the other end of the road.[6]

Years ago a newspaper headline appealed vividly to imagination and wonder. It seems that after four years of depression the real-estate men were faced in 1933, with the task of reappraising the entire world. The headline said, "Must Revalue Practically the Entire World." One had a mental picture of real-estate men going up and down all the streets of the world revaluing all the property, marking down new figures in little black books. What a fantastic idea! But how better could you describe what happens when one meets the Master in the community of faith? The whole world is revalued for the purposes of God's city, on account of God's children. The streets, the homes, the business and industry of a city or a nation are revalued in terms of what they do to people.

Third, some come seeking the Master in a community where his name is loved, persuaded that *they cannot really find him outside the family of believers.* "Where two or three are gathered together in my name," promised Jesus, "there am I in the midst of them." When I want most to see Jesus, I think it most likely that I shall find him where he said he would be, in the midst of those who take his name. It is not a question of not being able to see Christ anywhere, ever, outside this family. Who is to say where he may appear? Who could deny ever having met him in the solitude of some personal experience? But in his community of believers is his chosen dwelling. It was to a community of faith that Christ gave his last promise, "Go ye into all the world and teach all nations. . . . And I am with you always." It was upon a community of faith that God poured out His Holy Spirit at Pentecost. It was through the community of faith that God revealed Himself again and again when the vision faded—in the Revelation of John to the faithful under persecution, in the glorious hope of the City of God as it came to Augustine in the shadow of the descending darkness of the Middle Ages. It was through communities of faith that the evangelical renewals of the Reformation broke forth. And it is from a community of faith that the great Christian testimony of our own time comes forth—the united younger churches of the world and their startling witness to a oneness that transcends all barriers of race and nation.

Integrity forbids that we try to conceal or excuse the flaws or failures of the Christian Church down through the centuries. Christian people have fought each other in bitterness and blood. The followers of Christ have not hesitated to follow many crowds to do evil. They have taken the Lord's name in vain. But having said all of that, the undeniable fact remains that a new kind of people bears witness to a transforming power in the community of faith.

In Vincent McHugh's novel *The Victory*, one of the characters in describing some of the virtues that men had found amid the hideousness of war says, "There was the simple virtue of seriousness . . . good men doing their best . . . it was the guarantee that we had given to each other to keep the sky from falling." When people give that guarantee to each other, they give life a glory. Nothing is more glorious or transforming to see and to know than a faithful community of the followers of Christ "holding up the sky" for each other: standing strongly together so that he who stumbles does not fall, he who is afflicted is not crushed, he who is perplexed is not driven to despair, he who is persecuted is not forsaken, he who is struck down is not destroyed.

Albert Schweitzer tells us that he dedicated his life to "the fellowship of those who bear the marks of pain." As in no other place in the world, in the community of faith we discover where the fellowship of pain really is. Reflected from the cross is the pain of the world: the pain of man's sin, the pain of man's loneliness, the pain of man's grief. We find the company of those in pain both within the church and beyond its walls. And the community of faith is a community pledged to the love, healing, and redemption of people in every kind of pain, and more especially to those whose pain is suffered beyond the grasp of a beloved community of faith. No wonder we seek the company who call Christ Master. Outside this company we might miss altogether finding him who was acquainted with our grief, through whom we become acquainted with each other's grief, and by whose stripes we are healed.

IX

Long Night's Journey into Day

CHRIST, THE CONQUEROR OF OUR ANXIETY

BISHOP James Pike, of California, has written that millions of people wrestle with their inner problems without taking into account the fact of God. Such people, he says, are trying to put together a jigsaw puzzle with a good portion of the pieces missing from the set. In reading this, I remembered how once years ago my daughter and I had tried to put a jigsaw puzzle together. When we had used all the pieces we found we had a strange picture before us on the table. There were a lot of children rushing toward the center of the scene, but the center was missing. I seemed to recall the picture on the box that the puzzle originally came in—long since lost. There was a house, with a mother and father at the door, but this part of the picture was lost and those children were rushing toward an empty space. Perhaps this is a symbol of the way life seems to a multitude of people—a terrifying blank at the center where they look for security and hope. No house of security for the soul there; no God in whose love to find either purpose of peace. David Roberts summed it up: "Our age having dispensed almost entirely with the fear of God, now finds itself paralyzed with dread when it contemplates man and his power. And what makes this dread so acute is precisely the loss of faith; the sense that modern civilization has gone empty at the core."

In distress one man confessed to his minister, "I believe in God

—a God of law, moral laws, natural laws. Sometimes I think I believe in a personal God of love, but it's hard to hold on to him, and I get panicky, and I'm afraid I'm going to fail, and there is no faith to support me. What can I do?" All the way from this highly educated businessman to the gangs of youth on our city streets, this is the problem. Deeply disturbing is the epidemic of teen-age crime and juvenile delinquency in our great cities. From more than one professional source comes the diagnosis that this wave of unrest, breaking out in such frequent violence, is in no small measure the symptom of the deep anxiety of our age. These youngsters are the rootless generation persuaded that they have no future. Anxiety having been the climate of their home life from the beginning, their only true community the gang, they have no support for facing their world with either confidence or love.

Would it not be easy to imagine that these contemporaries follow in the procession led by the Greeks, who long ago came to Philip saying, "We would see Jesus"? In their train comes a mighty procession stretching across all the centuries. It includes the anxious, afraid, fearful men and women who ask above all else for assurance to conquer their anxiety. We all know at firsthand the many causes for fear: war, disease, failure, financial distress, loneliness, old age, death, the unknown. These are all legitimate, familiar apprehensions. In one form or another they lay siege to every one of us. But the great concern of those who seek Jesus, and those whose greatest, although unrecognized, need is to know Christ, is not so much with any of these specific worries and causes of fear, which can be appreciably alleviated by appropriate action. The burden with which they come is the general feeling of anxiety rising up out of the unconscious mind and often not attaching to anything in particular, a powerful and yet elusive fearfulness, a lack of confidence and trust toward life itself, a sense of having put their trust in something which ultimately cannot be trusted to sustain life. One of the ancient Psalmists has well described this feeling: "For the waters have come up to my neck. I sink in deep mire where there is no foothold. I have come into deep waters and the flood sweeps over me. I am weary with my crying, my throat is parched, my eyes grow dim with my waiting for God."

Some of this anxiety lies so deep that only medical therapy can reach it. Sometimes persons can take themselves in hand and allow healing to work. In either case, until faith takes hold, anxiety cannot be healed. Eugene O'Neill wrote a play with the intriguing title *Long Day's Journey into Night*. In the space of one day, by retrospect, he telescopes a family's deterioration and descent into gross darkness of sin and evil. All who suffer the acute distress of anxiety would describe themselves as in the passage of a long night. But with the companionship of Christ, it can be a *long night's journey into day*, for in him the dayspring from on high has visited us to give light to all who sit in darkness, even the fearsome darkness of anxiety. It was the poet W. H. Auden who called this "the age of anxiety." Few would take issue with the diagnosis. But if we sought Jesus in our anxiety what could he do for us? Can Christ truly be the conqueror of our anxiety? Would he write a prescription for our malady, or is there an antidote of faith that would come from him by contagion?

First, those who have ever seen the Master in their anxiety testify that he reminds us of *the great affirmatives of our faith*. We think and worry much about life's uncertainties: we take out insurance against the uncertain time of our death; we go for a medical checkup against the uncertain onset of disease; we subject ourselves to spiritual disciplines against the uncertainty of our moral strength or spiritual resources. And so we should. But what about life's certainties? Life has some immeasurable but massive certainties to set in the scale over against the uncertainties. Upon these we can support ourselves in any age.

"The earth is the Lord's and the fullness thereof, the world and they that dwell therein."

"God so loved the world that he gave his only begotten Son, that whosoever believeth on him shall not perish but have everlasting life."

"Nothing in all creation shall separate me from the love of God which is in Christ Jesus our Lord."

These are the strands of fabric from which the garment of faith is woven, and he who would keep anxiety under firm control must enfold himself within the mantle of these affirmations. These are the promises of God, and God has fulfilled these promises in the gift of His Son. God was in Christ. And what God did in Christ, He can do and will do for us. His incarnation in the midst of the life we live is witness that, come what may, God is able to overcome the world; that He is able to bring forth life out of death; that He is able to forgive sin and make all things new. These great affirmatives can put anxiety under firmer leash.

C. S. Lewis entitles his autobiography *Surprised by Joy*. To Lewis, the astounding effect of the gospel, when he finally accepted it, was the joy which he found. Wherever men have trustfully committed their lives to the good news, the gospel has had this same effect. Joy comes out of the discovery that, against everything that we or the circumstances of life have put or can ever put into one side of life's equation, God is never less than equal on the other. But Christ would have us live with these affirmatives, lean our minds and souls up against them day after day, week in and week out, one season to the next.

John Masefield tells us this revealing bit about one of the ways of his life:

For some years, at intervals, whenever life was not pressing too hard and making me too tired at the end of the day, I had practiced the getting of tranquility before going to sleep. I cannot recollect how this habit had begun but I had found the benefit of emptying the mind of worry whenever I turned in to my hammock on the *Conway*. Sometimes I had repeated the process in the early morning before turning out, so as to start the day with a quiet mind. The process was very simple. I read a page of thoughtful prose and then shutting my eyes, I repeated to myself a couple of poems, and then sang to myself—with mental voice—one, two, or even three or four songs. And usually before reaching the third or fourth, I had attained a mental quiet in which I could sort out the experiences of the day, annul its trouble as illusion and see its good. Often enough I did not attempt the process; sometimes it did not work, but when it did work it made me master of the day.[1]

How many Christians attempt this same process or anything like it, as a way to tranquility, or as a way to faith?

The writer of the 63rd Psalm has some words for us at this point: "My soul is feasted as with marrow and fat and my mouth praises thee with joyful lips when I think of thee upon my bed and meditate on thee in the watches of the night. For thou hast been my help and in the shadow of thy wings I sing for joy." Firmness of spirit comes to the person who takes his mind into this climate of affirmation. "Thou wilt keep him in perfect peace whose mind is stayed on thee."

Millions of people make it a nightly ritual to "catch the late news" on television before going to bed. How many of these people also make it a ritual to meditate upon God in the watches of the night? Or how many would say, if the truth were told,

> Now I lay me down to sleep,
> I've seen the news that would not keep,
> If I should die before I wake,
> At least I'll know what headlines make.

But when one has no more than the late news upon which to lean through the night of anxiety, the darkness goes on without end. Anyone who would make it a journey from night to day must do so on the strength of great affirmatives.

Christ can help in the passage from darkness to light, from anxiety to peace, by the reminder of what he was able to do for the anxious fears of his disciples. One time the disciples were in a boat on the Sea of Galilee when a sudden storm arose. They were seized with terror. Into the midst of their fears and through the midst of the storm's fury, Jesus came walking to them on the water. Who knows how Jesus walked on the water? By some optical illusion were the disciples deceived, or in the perfection of his life and faith could Jesus overcome the forces of nature which bound others? Of this we are not sure. However, he spoke to them saying, "Take heart, it is I, have no fear." Those words speak to my faith, saying that Christ comes to me, too. Through the storms that gather about my life—storms of fear, storms of inner wrestling with conscience, storms of temptation and shame—the Master comes saying the same words, "Take heart, it is I, have no fear." Then in the midst of this storm Peter cried out, "Lord, bid me to come to you on the waters." And Jesus bade him, "Come." Come across the deep water. And Peter set out to walk to Jesus. In the power of faith, I believe I can go where Christ calls me to go— whether to take up some burden of life or to lay it down; whether to face some lonely exile or to stand in some testing at the cross-roads. I believe God does not ask me to walk over deep waters where his arms of love will not reach out to hold. "Take heart, it is I, have no fear. Come."

Other great affirmatives rise up to stand against anxiety—those words from the 59th Psalm, "My God in his steadfast love will meet me." What strength and power in that word *steadfast!*—a love that is not moved, that abides and holds through all cir-cumstances. Then that verse from the 43rd chapter of Isaiah, "When you pass through the waters they shall not overwhelm you." All of these assurances are saying: as God takes our lives in His hands we become more than conquerors.

A wonderful phrase comes from Lytton Strachey's *Eminent Victorians.* In writing about General Gordon, he says, "The Sun-day before General Gordon started for the Sudan, he drove around London to a number of churches to take Communion as many times as possible, 'In order,' he said, 'to start thus brim full of God.'" Would six Communions in one day supply more of God than one Communion? Hardly. But to begin every day and every enterprise "brim full of God" because we have been with Christ, feeding upon the promises which God made—this is to be fortified in the conviction that there is more than a blank at the center of life.

Second, in the long passage from night to day is *the memory of God's providence*, the recollection of how God has been good to us and to those that we know. Even when adversity has brought us much sorrow, God has still been good to us if we will reckon the accounts aright. One of the last things that Amy Loveman wrote for the *Saturday Review* was a reflection on some words of Charles Poore, which appeared in the *New York Times Sunday Book Review*. Poore had remarked that time could be used more than once, particularly through memory. Amy Loveman added these thoughts, which go to the heart of our anxiety:

It is among the consolations of men in a distraught world that this should be so, that time can be used more than once. For it renders a man, to a degree, independent of the pressure of problems and possible catastrophe which conscript his thought in an age which is out of joint. It is not well, to be sure, to be a day dreamer—to walk with one's head in the clouds in a universe that is bristling with hard realities. This is the way of the escapist, and is not the way to usefulness or happiness. But to have a reservoir of memories, collective or individual, to fall back upon when disaster menaces, is to be fortified against despair and against anxiety. Both public and private health depend upon the resilience of mind that can see the present against the background of the past and project it against the future.[2]

In Charles Poore's wonderful phrase: "The balancing of time is inseparable from the art of living." The art of victorious living in this age of anxiety demands the balancing of time. "Jesus Christ, the same yesterday, today, and forever." I am sure that God has been good to me through Christ in the past. I may be sure that this same eternal God can be refuge to my children in the future and that underneath are the everlasting arms. Therefore, I can abide the present in the tension between these other two dimensions of time. I often think of Arthur Gossip's helpful way of putting it: "If we have the words of Jesus, we can endure his silence." His great words of promise surround his silence.

Yet there still come those in anxiety who say, "I must see Jesus, but I do not see him. And how can I believe? What good is living in a climate of affirmations to truth you cannot see or believe?" These questions are legitimate; faith that has neither wisdom nor art for the person in this darkness is a faith of small comfort. There are times for the arguments of philosophy; hardly is this one of them. Faith, however, has a wisdom that goes beyond philosophy. It calls us to live *as if* these promises were true. And the way to faith is not through argument but through experience. There are times when I cannot see but I will live *as if I have seen*. I may not be able to demonstrate that the earth is the Lord's, that God so loved the world that He gave His Son, that death shall not separate me from the love of God. I may not be able to demonstrate these, but by all the grace that is given me I will live as if these things were true.

Here we get a powerful assist from a simple conjunctive adverb that appears at a number of critical places in the New Testament. One of the most indispensable words in the vocabulary of faith is the adverb *nevertheless*. Sooner or later we all find ourselves in the teeth of some circumstances that cannot be moved, we find ourselves walking in some darkness through which we cannot see, we find ourselves threatened by some powers that must be resisted if we are to keep our souls. Then comes the moment to say, *nevertheless*. No matter what, we must go on our way to Jerusalem, as the Master declared when well-wishers warned him of Herod's threat. We must go on with life's purpose, which we once saw in green pastures and which still holds us now in dark valleys, though it be hidden from our sight.

Moreover, this word always begs to be spoken just at the point where life is most discouraging. Jesus one morning found the disciples in a boat a little way off from shore. They had toiled all night with the nets and caught no fish. Jesus said to them, "Let down your nets again." And Peter answered, "Master, we toiled all night and took nothing! Nevertheless at your word I will let down the nets." This is the place where you and I are likely to hear Christ speaking to us, saying the same words: "Let down your nets again."

I have toiled a long season at some hard task—and produced nothing. Nevertheless, at his word, I will let down the nets again into the same waters.

I have tried and tried to overcome some habit, or some temper, or some weakness—and succeeded at nothing. Nevertheless, at his word, I will try once more in the same waters.

I have labored in the best way I know to do what was right— and my best hopes all came to nothing. Nevertheless, at his word, I will labor on.

This is where faith meets its severest test, where we must go on without the tonic or the promise of victory in the thing at which we are engaged, without the support or the hope of security, without the guarantee that things will come the way we want them. For example, I do not want to submit to the disciplines that will take what seem to be life's most "rewarding" chances away from me. I do not want the risks of righteousness. I do not want the inconvenient necessities of doing what is right in race relations, in international relations, in all of my human relations. Nevertheless, if it be God's will for me to do these things I will submit to them. I do not want death to sever the bonds in which my life is held. Yet, if it must be, I will submit and accept it and let it serve the purposes of love. Who would suppose that a conjunctive adverb would be as uncomfortable as this one!

Yet here is a word with a strange and amazing power. For one thing it has the dogged power of determination. A man is strongly fortified if he can wake up in the morning ready to go into any day saying, "Nevertheless! Whatever I may be up against this day I will go on my way with integrity." That man has already settled the basic question: he is going to Jerusalem, come what may. He has no return ticket to Galilee in his pocket. It would seem to be a good exercise to put the word nevertheless where we can see it every morning when we awake. Furthermore, this word has the contagion of Jesus' own power in it. When we come to the crossroads where bitter decisions await to be made, and when we stand under that stern imperative we cannot avoid without losing our souls, it is a comfort to know that the Master has gone this way before us, and that before us he said, *nevertheless!*

Whether I can reason it all out or not, in any case I am going on the assumption that the fruits of faith are better than the harvest of doubt. Moreover, I am going on the assumption that actually to live the faith is the best way to open my eyes and persuade me of its truth. I remember the excitement of approaching the steps leading into York Minster in England. Looking up at the huge window in the west face of the cathedral, I could not believe that the seemingly drab, dingy glass contained any color. Was this the rose window of which men had written in such rapture? Then I went through the great doors, walked far down the nave to the chancel steps, and turned toward the window. The afternoon sun streaming *through* the stained glass transformed the window to colors and patterns more beautiful than I had ever seen or imagined. But I had to stand at the heart of the cathedral to see them. So it is with faith. One has to stand at the heart of faith to know the support of God's love.

Moreover, if Christ would conquer anxiety, he insists that we stand together in the support of affection and concern for one another. We live in a time when it is not good for a man to be alone. Christ can be the conqueror of our anxiety only as he leads us to steady and support others who draw their strength from us. There is a magnificent prayer in that same 69th Psalm which began with those words of overwhelming lament from the man whose eyes had grown dim from waiting for God. But this Psalmist goes on to pray, "Let not those who hope in thee be put to shame through me, O Lord God of Hosts. Let not those who seek thee be brought to dishonor through me, O Lord God of Israel." Someone is depending upon me not to be anxious. For his sake, for her sake, I consecrate myself. With God's help I will stand against anxiety and be a tower of strength to my dependents.

Now let us be clear in distinguishing this life of faith from another kind of so-called "peaceful living" much sought after in these days of anxiety. Peer Gynt described the latter on hearing a kindly sermon over a dead man of ugly reputation when he said, "Well, that's what I call Christianity. Nothing in it to make one feel uneasy." There is plenty in the gospel to make one feel uneasy, and anyone who reads the whole gospel soon discovers that it is Christ's purpose to *make* us feel uneasy even in this age of anxiety—uneasy about ourselves and uneasy about our world. But this is not the uneasiness of the fretful self-concern spun out of anxiety for our own happiness. It is uneasiness growing out of concern for God's holiness. And this is a vastly different thing. Faith is always a risk, and Christ does not remove that risk. Faith almost guarantees that you will suffer. And even the Son of man must suffer many things and be killed. The gospel offers no peace-of-mind guarantee. The security patterns of our fond imagination do not hold up in the face of the gospel. The Greeks had a word for this kind of freedom from emotion. It was the word *apathy*—undisturbedness. This is not what Christ offers to any man. Indeed the opposite: "In the world you shall have tribulation." Christ offers instead the promise to make life new. Regeneration always involves a revolution. He offers to forgive sin and raise us to eternal life—and penitence always sends us through pain. But all the time he offers to be with us. "And his name shall be called Emmanuel because he is God with us." The conviction of these things makes a vital difference: that God is in the midst of His creation, that He does care what happens now and forever, that our lives were made not for the endurance of any human failure or the destiny of any human evil but for eternity. Christ was born for this. We would see *this* Jesus!

An early Christian martyr in the Roman arena voiced his faith saying, "Far above this darksome circus still shine the stars." How did the early Christians ever get through their age of anxiety? As James Reid has put it, "They got through it all because they saw through it all. They saw through it to another world." And this was not pie in the sky when you die, but the recognition that God has given life a glory and because He has given life a glory, because He has made it for Himself both now and forever, this life is worth living victoriously. And more than that—it is possible to live it victoriously.

Warwick Deeping, in his novel *The Road*, tells of an ex-officer who in any moral crisis, when life seemed to be so twisted by evil, so mean and crushed by misfortune, that it looked as though it could not be retrieved, always recalled himself and others, and rallied them with the words "Christ is risen, Christ is risen." This idea he kept repeating in desperate moments as a guarantee of recovery and victory. For the Resurrection is God's power for repair available to all broken lives and all hearts that are full of anxiety. Be not anxious. The thing that redeems those words from being mere hollow advice is this: that the One who said them was the One who also said, "I am the Resurrection and the Life." And he was the One who rose victorious over sin and death.

X

For Such a King We've Waited All Our Life

CHRIST, THE SAVIOUR OF THE WORLD

THESE are the words of Dr. Warren Weaver, Vice-President for the Natural and Medical Sciences, the Rockefeller Foundation:

It was Christmas Eve nearly twenty centuries ago. A strange new star was in the sky on that wondrous night in Judea. The wise men followed it from afar and came to worship. These troubled nights before Christmas 1957, strange new stars have appeared in our sky. We have followed them with radio, and we are uncertain at the moment as to just who or where the wise men are. . . . For gentle and lovely reasons, the world was a new place after the appearance of the star of Bethlehem. For rude and terrifying reasons, the world is again a new place, following the launching of the metallic stars that have been streaking across our dawn and twilight sky. Silent Night, Holy Night the choristers sing. But it hasn't been silent on 20.005 and 40.002 megacycles. And how are we going to keep it holy?[1]

"We are not sure just who or where the wise men are"? Or if there is any hope for our world!

When Stanley found Livingstone in the African wilderness, he gave him the letters he had brought, and said to Livingstone, "Read your letters from home first; you must be impatient for them."

"Ah," replied Livingstone, "I have waited for years for letters, I can wait a few hours more. No, tell me first, how is the world getting along?"

Over the minds and hearts of multitudes of people throughout the world this question hovers like a great pall: how is the world getting on? As one writer put it: "Above us the constant threat of war so awful, so universal, so destructive as would lay the planet waste in horror . . . around us millions who are permanently hungry, millions who are slaves in labor camps or prisons, slums, slavery, destitution, frustration and appalling boredom." Is God to save us from all this? What hope is there for the world? When we have found faith in eternal life, when faith has put personal anxiety on leash, even when we have experienced God's saving love to redeem our own lives from sin, there remains this vast unknown—can the world be saved? Many come with the Greeks saying, "We would see Jesus" to find answer to this question: does Christ offer any saving gospel to the world?

We start with the faith of scripture. Here is the writer of the 67th Psalm:

> May God be gracious to us and bless us
> And make his face to shine upon us
> That thy ways may be known upon earth
> Thy *saving power* among all nations.

Said the Second Isaiah, "The Lord has bared his holy arm before the eyes of all the nations; and all the ends of the earth shall see the salvation of our God." It is the conviction of the writer of the Fourth Gospel that "This is indeed Christ, the Saviour of the world." The writer of the First Epistle of John put it this way: "The Father sent the Son to be the Saviour of the world." And the very first words of the gospel are these: "And Jesus began to preach saying, 'repent, for the kingdom of heaven is at hand.' "

This is the faith of the Scriptures: God will be the Saviour of the world. Many in our time have come to doubt that faith. The terrifying events of the last fifty years have shaken the easy confidence that men recently had in the salvation of the world. The Kingdom of God on earth was coming closer and closer. What a hollow sound that confidence has now! In reaction to World War

I and World War II, the Korean War, the Russian Revolution, the Chinese Revolution, the ordeal of Nazi Germany, race conflicts all over the earth, men have grown discouraged, pessimistic, and cynical. Millions have given up faith in God altogether. The Archbishop of Canterbury said some time ago, "For the first time since Christianity was brought to Great Britain the great majority of its people look upon religion as something irrelevant to their lives."

Is it irrelevant? Have the disastrous events of this century rendered the whole gospel of salvation null and void, demonstrated that Christ, the hope of the world, is a vain hope? Before answer can be given to that question there needs to be some clearing away of the undergrowth of superstition. To begin with, the saving of Western civilization and "saving the world" by Christ are not synonymous! Toynbee has summed it up in a sentence: "We can be sure that Western civilization's role in history is going to be a minor role compared with the role of Christianity." That Toynbee said it does not necessarily make it true, but prophetic religion has always given a sharp warning that only a redeemed civilization can stand in the day of judgment. Like all civilizations before it, our civilization has within it the seeds of its own destruction and they are the same seeds that have flourished in every other civilization the world has known. Unless these seeds be radically redeemed by some ultimate vision, or power beyond itself, we cannot expect it to be any more tolerable for us than it was for Tyre or Sidon, Babylon or Rome. Prophetic religion is clear about another point: God's salvation has a wider purpose and destiny than the perpetuation of the American way, or Western civilization, or some fragmentary way-station in the historical process. If what we are looking for is victory in the cold war, then Christ, Saviour of the world, is quite irrelevant to that.

There is yet another dense tangle through which we have to cut a path in seeking Christ, the Saviour, and that is the problem raised by the immoral contradictions of justice in the world. The writer of the 73rd Psalm faced this incongruity:

But as for me, my feet had almost stumbled,
    my steps had well nigh slipped.
For I was envious of the arrogant, when I
    saw the prosperity of the wicked.

For they have no pang;
    their bodies are sound and sleek.
They are not in trouble as other men are;
    they are not stricken like other men.

In the working out of God's saving strategy, whatever the design
may be, one fact is obvious: God does not pay His moral wages
every Saturday night. The centuries may bring God's recompense
for evil (although even this is far from clear), but certainly no
man is promised a quick profit on his investment of righteousness.
We are on demonstrably safer ground when we appeal to the
claim that *in the long run* it goes well with good and ill with wickedness. This, to be sure, raises questions about the justice to those
who receive no promises while the "long run" is going on. Neither
must we confuse the "long run" with the "escalator." God's salvation of the world is not the gradual process by which everything
gets better and better. If there were any such process many would
say that somehow it has gone into reverse and that everything is
rapidly getting worse and worse. In any case Christ, the Saviour
of the world, offers no neat balance of moral rewards or recompense. The Christian religion will always seem irrelevant to those
who seek salvation of the whole of life in some fragment of life.
Reinhold Niebuhr has pointed out that disillusionment is twice
compounded, for secular man is now finding out that "our
gadget-filled paradise suspended in a hell of international insecurity certainly does not offer us even the happiness of which the
former century dreamed."

Our seeking runs through another tangled patch of confusion.
There are many people for whom the gospel of Christ is both
solace and inspiration for their own inner life and in their personal
relationships one with another, but who look upon it as altogether

irrelevant and "impractical" as a way of saving the world. They go
the second mile, they turn the other cheek, they forgive the people
who despitefully use them in the personal relationships of life, but,
they say, this is much too idealistic a way to run a business or to
solve the problems of government. It's impractical; it won't work.
Insofar as man's personal life is concerned, the Kingdom of heaven
may belong to the poor in spirit, and in some distant heaven great
may be the reward of those who are persecuted for righteousness'
sake, but in this world the meek do not inherit the earth, and
turning the other cheek to Communism is most impractical. So
the argument runs. And perhaps the argument may not be far
wrong. We have to reckon with the fact that groups of people—
committees, nations, races—are disposed toward sin and unrighteousness in the same way that individuals are. Along with man's
idealism and all the good that men have done in the world, as
though running on a parallel track is man's perversity and his
evil intentions. Moreover, forgiveness and reconciliation may be a
simple possibility between my neighbor and myself, even when
my neighbor is a Russian Communist or a member of a colored
race. But forgiveness and reconciliation are not simple possibilities
between America and Russia, between the white race and the colored. More than that, it is an undeniable fact that men will consent to sin in communities in a way that they would never toler-
ate as individuals. Consider the silent Germans who stood by
watching the Nazi mobs loot and burn and kill. Taken one by
one, these silent watchers would never have consented to such
evil. Or consider the great numbers of "respectable, righteous"
persons who break the hearts of people in the minority groups of
this land by all kinds of restrictive covenants forcing them into
second-class citizenship. As person to person we would never hu-
miliate another human being the way we persecute him in the
impersonal social mass. These are the obstinate unyielding facts
of social sin, and any answer to our question will have to deal
with these ugly realities. Is our gospel then unrealistic, impractical,
and irrelevant? How does Christ become the Saviour, even Saviour

for the stubborn afflictions of mankind and the evils which trouble the world's peace? We can answer this question if we see Christ as Saviour in two dimensions of his saving power, one immediate, one eternal.

First, Christ is Saviour of the world *now* because in him we find the spirit of reconciliation, the abundance of God's grace by which both justice and mercy may work for the healing of mankind. God has made of one blood all nations of men. He is the God and Father of all mankind. But we are divided from one another by animosities of race, by pride of nation. We are alien to one another in seeking each for his private security. The human family is torn asunder by sin. In ourselves we cannot find the way to overcome our separation from each other and from God. As the Prayer Book has it, ". . . there is no health in us," which is to say, saving power is not in ourselves. But in the spirit of reconciliation which God revealed to the world in Jesus Christ is a temper, a way, a power through which men may be reconciled, their separation overcome, through which good will may heal the hurts of sin.

Again let us be clear in what we say. Not that Christ makes international good will a sudden simple possibility. Not that he offers some easy immediate way to end race conflict. But rather that in the spirit of Christ is both incentive and resource to redeem some present community, to take some immediate step, to prevent some tragic moral disaster—things which might not be done *apart from a grace beyond ourselves in him*. What we are saying here is that God disclosed in the life, death, and resurrection of Christ a redeeming power and a reconciling love that rescue man's history from devolving in cycles of hopeless futility. It has been demonstrated in Christ that from the descent into any darkness *the way can be turned*. The Christian way of forbearance and forgiveness, the walking in lowly paths of service, the loyalty to high demands of justice, can and do redeem life where they are attempted. In age after age across the Christian centuries innumerable dark corners have been redeemed by men and women who believed in the good

news and who trusted it in the ordering of their lives, and the
lives of the societies and communities of which they were a part.

William Penn and Roger Williams trusted the gospel in colonial
America and made Pennsylvania and Rhode Island sanctuaries
of sanity, tolerance, brotherhood, and good will in the midst of
cruelty, arrogance, and parochialism. The people called Metho-
dists trusted the gospel in eighteenth-century England. Their
faithfulness to discipline, temperance, and justice in significant
measure transformed and redeemed the rotten, festering life of
those cities of human degradation and neglect. Martin Luther
King and the Negroes trusted the gospel in Montgomery, Ala-
bama, when they met injustice with forgiveness and non-violent
resistance to ill treatment and discrimination. The life of that city
was redeemed to at least a closer approximation of Christian
righteousness and mercy. And although the United Nations has
not abolished war, nor in its present form can hope to abolish it,
at least those who founded the United Nations, believing that some
kind of internationalism was the only hope of the world, gave
mankind a better opportunity to prevent war, to relieve suffering, to mediate disputes, and to establish justice among the nations.

We could go on and on. In industrial management, in business
affairs, in labor relations, men have—in one place after another—
believed that we are our brother's keeper, that we ought to bear
one another's burdens, that we should do to others what we would
want them to do to us, and that he who would be great among us
must be the servant of all. And believing these things, men have
tried them, and by trying them have reclaimed communities and
brought even to whole nations a greater measure of freedom and
justice. Contrast the vindictive peace treaties of 1871 and 1919
with the spirit which informed our relations with Germany and
Japan in 1945 and the years following. No one would claim that
we had fashioned the perfect instrument of peace, or that America
and Japan are altogether reconciled. But peace and justice have
more of a chance now than they did formerly.

The Christian does not say that because of the gospel the world is getting better. He does claim there is a saving power in the gospel wherever men trust it to transform an evil present to a hopeful future. Were it not for the effect of Christian restraint, the influence of Christian behavior, the grace to do justly while we love mercy, even when this is mixed with impure and selfish motives, life would be altogether insufferable. We are talking here about a grace and a spirit of reconciliation that is in the spirit of Christ, even where it does not bear the Christian label. We find that spirit in One whom we call Saviour.

Second, beyond this present, Christ is also the ultimate Saviour of the world because the cross offers man an eternal and unshakable hope against the despair and defeats of history. In the drama of the Crucifixion God gave demonstration of both His purpose and His power to contend against the principalities and powers of darkness which destroy us. The cross itself sinks us into despair. Richard Jefferies relates the incident of a boy who was reading the story of the Crucifixion: "The Crucifixion hurt his feelings very much— the cruel nails; the unfeeling spear; he looked at the picture a long time and then turned the page saying, 'If God had been there he would not have let them do it.'" Looking at so many of the hideous evils of the world, we are tempted to say the same thing— if God had been there, these would not have happened. But the gospel tells us that God was there, and that this very cross was His instrument by which He came with power to save. In the conviction that God defeated the evil powers of sin in the conquest of the cross, Christians have faced life believing that God's ultimate victory is assured. Said Paul, in his letter to the Colossians, "God disarmed the principalities and powers and made a public example of them, triumphing over them in Christ." James Stewart sums it up this way: "God made a show of the powers of evil and darkness and at Calvary he put them to rout." All of the diabolical force of men in the world was hurled against God in the attempt to destroy Christ. That attempt failed: it failed to destroy his love, to put out his light, to bury his life. Henceforth we know that sin and darkness are not the ruling powers of the universe. God has measured them and conquered them.

It was reported by a Dutch friend that in 1940, once the battle of Britain had been won, people in Holland were convinced that Germany could not win the war, that Germany in principle was beaten. There might be long and terrible years of endurance before the final victory; they themselves might very probably not live to see their country delivered from the oppressor, but the final result was certain! This was not just a victory to be shared by the generation who happened to be living when the end came. This was victory that belonged to the whole nation, even to these whose lives were lived during the kingdom of oppression. They, too, belonged to Holland. To a greater Holland, to a Holland greater than Hitler. And even by their sorrow and sacrifice they found their truest citizenship in this greater Holland. In the same way Christian disciples devoted to God's Kingdom labor here for the "progress of knowledge, the promotion of justice, the reign of peace, and the realization of human brotherhood," not as though they were fighting a rear-guard action in some hopeless lost cause, but fully persuaded that the triumph of righteousness belongs to God's design for the world, even though they may not live to see that final fulfillment. And in this struggle which remains, men take heart and find hope in belonging to the faith and in being possessed by the gospel.

Here is a quotation from the diary of Lord Ashley, the seventh Earl of Shaftesbury, who did so much for the social redemption of England in the nineteenth century:

Last night defeated—utterly, singularly, prodigiously defeated by a majority of 138! . . . "Cast down but not destroyed." I feel no abatement of faith, no sinking of hope, no relaxation of perseverance. The stillest and darkest hour of night precedes the dawn. "Though it tarry, wait for it," believing that God sends you a trial and yet bears you up with a corresponding courage; and, although you may pass not the stream of Jordan, it is something that God has permitted you to wash your feet in the waters of the Promised Land.[2]

There is a saving power in hope when it thus sustains a man, or a church, or a community. We have always before us the long hope for God's righteousness. In this hope is no promise that everything is automatically going to be all right. Civilization can be lost. Nations can be defeated. Our faith is not that Western civilization is indestructible but rather that the righteousness of God cannot be finally overwhelmed by the defeat of any civilization. This is the faith of the Scriptures, which say that the kingdoms of this world are become the Kingdom of our Lord and of His Christ.

Will this come for our children's children or some far-off generation to see on earth? Or will nuclear warfare and radiation put an end to all men's hopes in the death of all life upon the planet? The answer to these questions is not in the gospel, nor are we supposed to know the answer. "It is not for you to know the times and seasons, which the Father has put in his own power." We had best remember Jesus' words to Peter, who asked him after the Resurrection, referring to John, "What about this man?" And Jesus said to Peter, "What is that to you? Follow me." We have one duty, and that is to follow Christ and take the gospel into the midst of the life that we know. The threat of destruction by nuclear power is menacing, to be sure. But does it alter the prospect which we have always faced? Man has known—at least since the dawn of the scientific age—that some day the world and all its life would pass away. Christ, Saviour of the world, certainly must offer some hope beyond the prospect of a final harmony on earth (for a fortunate few living at the end of time!), to be frozen out in the flicker of a dying sun. His Kingdom will, in some unknown measure, lie in this world. But his Kingdom is ultimately a Kingdom beyond this world. Those who enter his Kingdom, even here and now, enter also that Kingdom which cannot be shaken.

In Gian-Carlo Menotti's opera *Amahl and the Night Visitors* there is a tremendous line spoken by the mother. The three kings, on their way to Bethlehem, visit the mother and her crippled child.

They tell them of the great King whose birth has called them to journey. On hearing of him, the mother says in wonder, *"For such a King I've been waiting all my life."* Indeed, for such a King and Saviour, the world has been waiting all of its life. The good news is that such a King has come and waits for us now.

Living in Two Worlds at Once

CHRIST, THE RISEN LORD

"FATHER of spirits, we thank thee for the dear and holy dead, who compass us as a cloud of witnesses, and make the distant heaven a home to our hearts."

"Assist us to return to the scenes of our daily life."

These two prayers, taken from the orders for the burial of the dead, hold in tension the necessity which Christ lays upon us all—that we live in two worlds at the same time: that we live among the scenes of our daily life, but that we also make the distant heaven a home for our hearts. If we are to do this we must see Christ as our risen Lord. We must see him both as one who still meets us in the familiar places of our dwelling and as one whose kingdom is not of this world.

"If Christ be not risen from the dead, then your faith is in vain!" These are the decisive words of Paul to the Corinthians, and they pin the whole structure of Christian assurance on the central fact of the resurrection of Jesus Christ. If Jesus Christ was not raised from the dead, then the whole house of faith comes tumbling down. The good news, however, is that Christ has been raised from the dead. As risen Lord he does come to the places in our lives where we need him most.

First, we need to meet Jesus as risen Lord wherever we face *the aggressive challenge of a secular world* that leaves God out, a world that puts all the pieces of life's puzzle together and lo,

123

God is not in the picture. He is not there because the puzzle is complete without Him. Or, more truthfully, there is no puzzle to which God could provide the solution. There are no empty spaces which God might occupy.

Moreover, we do not need to go to Moscow to face this challenge and denial. In 1938 Dr. J. S. Whale, of Cambridge University, received a letter from a radio listener in Yorkshire who had heard one of his talks on religion over the BBC. This is what the stranger wrote:

I am sixty-five years of age, retired after an active life and very happy. My wife is six months younger than me. We have been married forty years very happily. We have never attended church. We have never said a prayer. We neither of us believe in life after death. We believe in making this world better. Without being egotistical, I believe we have succeeded. We are highly respected by our neighbors. We are not hampered by creeds, but stare life squarely in the face. You might, in your talks, tell me what religion has to offer us.[1]

Now let it be said that this man is not an unusual creature. His name is legion. You will meet him on every street. Religion would have, in his words, a number of things to offer to this man, the first of which might well be these words of William Lawrence Sullivan:

Be a materialist, an atheist if you must. But open your eyes to all that it means. It means that you have no organic connection with mankind; that you are standing on air; that you are alien to the greatest art and profoundest experiences in history; that you have adopted a cause which, from having no past, can have no future; that you must ignore or suppress the deepest and most prophetic impulsions of your inner life; that you must accept as the fundamental tone and rhythm of your existence a tragic pathos that can never rise to victorious confidence or pure joy; and that you must regard the whole universe as a paradoxical imposture—a homeless home, a discordant order, a lawless abode of law, a systematic incoherence, a wandering without a destination, an ideal fashioner without an ideal, a reach with nothing to grasp, links but not a chain, an unintelligent basis of

all our intelligence, the blind bestower of all our seeing! If in sheer
mental comfort and accommodation you find it easier to believe all
that than to believe in Sovereign Spirit, no man can say you Nay—but
do not expect the outraged universe to answer Yes.

Now to be sure, this does not tell our inquiring friend what
religion has to offer him, but it does something even preliminary
to that: it points out to him what he casts aside in his denial. He
ought at least to know exactly where he stands. And beyond
this, as he is staring life squarely in the face, he ought to see the
full implications of where humanistic denial may lead. It might
help him to hear the words of a young Chinese Communist:

Now I am no longer the former man you knew. Apart from my body
which is the same, my whole mind and thought have changed. I have
become a new man in the classless revolution pioneer corps, a loyal
believer of Marx-Leninism. I shall never live for myself alone but for
the masses. What satisfies my aspiration now is the progress of a
happy socialism to a communist state. In this new teaching I have
found unimagined blessing and happiness. I am very sorry, but I must
inform you that I no longer believe in God nor worship him. I can no
longer address you as a religious brother, but I send you my revolution-
ary love.

As opposed to the Communist, the polite Yorkshireman certainly is on the side of the angels. But, however high-minded his
ideal may be and however sincere his devotion to making this a
better world, he is overmatched and underprepared to face the
challenge of a thoroughgoing materialism like that, a materialism
that carries to the limit the implications of its claims about life.
Like the Communist, like the aggressive materialist, this debonair
humanist with his affable complacency has given up his belief in
God, a God who has come into the world to give eternal validation
and power to his values. This man's values—even for making the
world better—are all humanly derived. But if they are no more
than humanly inspired and supported, impersonally spiritual at
best, then they are no better than the men who make them, who

support them, and they lay no claim upon us beyond the fashion of the time. And as F. W. H. Meyers suggested, one does not escape the pit by spelling humanity with a capital "H." It was the Archbishop of York who put it so well many years ago: "There can be no new order without new men, no new earth without new heavens, no new world if we use for building material the old worldliness."

What difference, then, does it make if we see Jesus as risen Lord? It makes this difference: if Christ be risen from the dead, we have testament from God Himself to a power stronger than death, a power able to overcome evil, the witness that the mundane affairs of our life have importance to God who inhabits eternity, and that evil has met its match in him who "lived and died and rose again and liveth evermore." Sir Arnold Toynbee has expressed the implications of this for the world situation:

We cannot meet the Communist challenge on this secular ground, but only on the Israelite belief that individual human souls have been created by God and have supreme value in his eyes, and from the Christian additional belief that God has demonstrated his love for human souls by redeeming them through a supreme act of self-sacrifice. These foundations are not just theological propositions; they are a vision of God's nature and man's destiny that can inspire us, with God's help, to lead a new life.[2]

Surely one can see the nobility of life through secular eyes, as the Stoics and others have done. And even if life had no destiny beyond the grave, even if this world were no outpost of a greater Kingdom beyond, but merely a lost island in a friendless universe, even then one might still say, "While I have breath in my body I will love life—my righteousness I will hold fast." So far so good. But what does one do when he stands in the face of enormous evil and crushing power? Man standing in his own naked power is not sufficient for these things, for man left to his own devices devises evil. But if Christ be risen from the dead, then, as Karl Barth has put it, "History is illuminated from beyond the frontier of history." I can face the Communist challenge, I can face the challenge of a heedless, grasping way of life in the sureness that the vast resources of God have moved across the frontier of history and are thrown into the struggle. This does not guarantee any visible victory tomorrow. It does give me new eyes to see, "not just all around this present age but beyond it"; it does give me the joy of finding our destiny and strength in a world beyond, and finding it gives me courage to face the world of here and now; it does give me the comfort of One who stands beside us in concern for ultimate justice, for everlasting mercy, and for eternal truth; it does offer hope that, however costly the long warfare, God has not been and will not be defeated.

Second, we need to meet Jesus as risen Lord when we stand *in the ruins of our defeats and in the shadow of our death*. Held fast by sin and bound by the fear of death, we need the risen Christ to bear the report of his victory. In one of the great Christmas hymns of our liturgy are the words, "good Christian men, rejoice." But what do the words "good Christian men, rejoice" mean when they are spoken in the face of death? Both life and death are frightening in their prospect when we imagine that we face them all alone. In her book called *The White Gate: Adventures in the Imagination of a Child*, Mary Ellen Chase recalls for us a vivid dream which recurred regularly throughout her childhood. It may profit us to consider her dream in detail because it seems to be a sharp, vivid symbol of the fears we all harbor:

I dreamed that I was alone on some immeasurably vast plain. Beside me there was no one and nothing. The plain, which was everything and everywhere, seemed to be made of white particles, like crystals, which held neither light nor heat nor cold and which seemed to be like rock salt, used to freeze our ice-cream in the summer. Over this limitless white expanse there lay a heavy drifting mist, also white, which concealed the sky, if there was a sky. There was nothing visible on this endless waste, not a tree, or a rock, or even a hill. It was completely boundless and flat, and I somehow knew that far beyond the reach of my eyes it was the same.

In this dream I walked across this desolate expanse in a strange
obscurity, neither dark nor light. And even more terrifying than the
dimness, the utter silence, and the vastness was the understanding that
I must walk alone forever there, for not only could I make no progress,
but there was no end to reach. At every step through the white
substance my heavy, tired feet sank deeper within it until I thought
that I could not draw them out, that at last my whole body would be
out of sight, and that I must finally be lost in nothing at all. At every
step, too, I looked back to see the impression of my footprints in the
white crystals, but they were never there. Even this sign of me and of
my endless journey had disappeared.

. . . This dream became my terror by night. . . . Always the
empty, white, endless plain; the silence; the half-light; the weight of
my sinking feet; the knowledge that I am abandoned, helpless, alone,
and that at last I must become nothing at all.[3]

That dream is a symbol of the fears of men, the fear that we
are alone, that we have been abandoned, that we are helpless,
and that at last we must become nothing at all. Such a dream
overshadows the heart and soul of every one of us. Unless across
the empty white endless plain Jesus comes to us as risen Lord, we
are without hope, and have

> Neither joy, nor love, nor light,
> Nor certitude, nor peace, nor help for pain.

Unless we see Jesus as risen Lord, we must do as the small boy
did who cast himself on his brother's grave, listened, and then
said: "It's all quiet." So it always is in nature's silence—if Christ
be not risen from the dead.

But that Christ is risen from the dead makes all the difference
how we stand in the daily defeats of life, and how we stand before
the final denial in this world. To see Jesus as risen Lord arms us
with faith sufficient to abide even the most distressing denials
which life brings. This is what John Winthrop wrote to his wife
before he sailed from England to Massachusetts Bay on the
Arbella:

I shall yet againe see thy sweet face in the land of the livinge—
that lovely countenance, that I have so much delighted in, and beheld
with so great contente! . . . I hope, the course we have agreed upon
will be some ease to us both. mundays and frydays, at 5: of the clock
at night, we shall meet in spiritt till we meet in person. yet, if all these
hopes should faile, blessed be our God, that we are assured we shall
meet one day, if not as husband and wife, yet in a better condition,
let that staye and comfort thy heart. neither can the sea drowne thy
husband, nor enemyes destroy, nor any adversity deprive thee of thy
husband or children. therefore I will onley take thee now and my sweet
children in mine arms, and kiss and embrace you all, and so leave you
with my God. Farewell, farewell. . . .

Because Christ brought life and immortality to light through
the gospel, John Winthrop could write those words with assurance.
Because people have walked with a risen Lord in this life, they
fear no frontier at the end of this life, for there is One who can
lead them across all frontiers, who gives them even now citizenship
in two worlds.

Robert MacAfee Brown writes that shortly after the death of
Dean David Roberts, of Union Theological Seminary, Brown's
three-and-a-half-year-old boy was asking why he wouldn't see
"Wendy's daddy" any more. Young Mark Brown was perplexed
and a bit indignant about what had happened to Dave Roberts.
But his father says: "When my wife told him that Wendy's daddy
was with God, Mark replied in tones of infinite acceptance and
understanding, 'Oh! Then he's still real.' " How could we say it
any better than Mark said it: "Then he is still real"? Except for
the risen Lord, how would we know that Dave or anyone else is
still real? But those who live with the risen Christ in this world
live also in that other world which even death does not destroy.
In this faith we may pray with all confidence in the words of
Lucy Whitmell as she expresses it in her "Christ in Flanders":

> Though we forget You—You will not forget us—
> We feel so sure that You will not forget us—
> But stay with us until this dream is past.

And so we ask for courage, strength, and pardon—
Especially, I think, we ask for pardon—
And that You'll stand beside us to the last.[4]

Third, we need to meet Jesus as risen Lord in the *mundane
disciplines of daily living.* Ordinarily we feel little sense of crisis
about these disciplines; for that reason they may seem quite unre-
lated to the risen Lord. Standing beside an open grave we are
overwhelmned with the consequences—"If Christ be not risen
from the dead." But sitting down to the distasteful work of a Monday morning we are likely not even to think of the Resurrection.
And inevitably with disastrous results! For this reason: if Christ
be not risen from the dead, then the details of a Monday morning
will add up to one kind of sum. But if Christ meets us as risen
Lord, their sum will be something altogether different. This may
be happening quite unconsciously. It was William Ernest Hocking
who reminded us: "The cause of the trouble is that while the
pleasurable spots in our lives are numerous and details have
specific purposes, we are without a sense of the significance and
purpose of life as a whole. When the whole is left without meaning
and objective its parts must lose their worth." This process can
wear our lives out while we never know what's happening. With
no meaning from beyond life held at the center of life, no eternal
purpose lifting life up to dwell in a world beyond all visible and
temporal aspects, no experience of the eternal made manifest
in time, the details of existence will have no dimensions beyond
momentary episodes. We may not consciously reason this all out in
any logical way, but subconsciously we realize in our hearts that
life's sum is zero. When the resurrection faith is taken away,
the whole is left without meaning. The trouble is that we are
trying to make ourselves completely at home in this world and
we cannot. For this world is but a fragment of our whole life, and
we cannot find a whole meaning in a fragment.

On the other hand, when we come to the affairs of any day in
the sure consciousness that these affairs belong not alone to us to
order and dispose once and for all, but also to One to whom we

belong, both now and forever, we see them with new eyes. Each act then has consequences unto eternity. The composer Robert Schumann once said: "I always play as if a master were listening."

Here is a man going about the tedious tasks of a routine job. Will it make but little difference to him whether he faces these tasks as simply "one damn thing after another" or whether he "plays" them as if a risen Master were listening? In the one case he will be concerned only to get through with them as speedily as possible. In the other, he will be concerned how he performs them—and whether they are "played" to the everlasting glory of God. With the risen Christ the "humblest work will shine and the roughest places be made plain."

Here is a woman whose shining hopes have lost their luster, whose life stretches out now in unrelieved monotony, "tomorrow and tomorrow and tomorrow"! Will it make but little difference to her whether she walks these days alone to nothingness or whether she can "play" them as if a risen Master were listening, knowing that his ear is tuned for how she strikes each note and not what she plays?

> Now that the King has gone this way,
> Great are the things of every day.

See how this works out in a life thoroughly beset by monotony and severe testing. Thus writes Alice Freeman Palmer, whose sister was seriously ill and who, her financial prospects growing steadily darker, was herself recovering from a severe sickness: "You ask me if I am happy. Let me be honest with you tonight. No, I am not. But I am content, and that is better. I am at work, and before me stretch high aims and great tasks, more than enough to fill the years until I shall awake in His likeness and be satisfied." This is the consequence of facing the march of days in company with a risen Lord: *high aims, great tasks, contentment* in the midst of strife. All of these and more we have when we trust life to One who conquered death.

Moreover, not only does the ordinary become the extraordinary, but the reverse is also true: what had seemed extraordinary now appears quite ordinary. In T. S. Eliot's play *Family Reunion*, one of the characters says of Harry: "Harry has crossed the frontier beyond which danger and safety have a different meaning. Death is now only on this side." Any day which begins with reassurance of the risen Christ may indeed have its episodes of what we call danger, but the whole idea of safety and danger will be altogether different. It will at last be plain that we are really safe only when we are doing the will of him who is Lord and Master. To know this is to have crossed the frontier between two worlds.

Said Dorothy Sayers: "If Christ could take evil and suffering and do that sort of thing with them, then of course it is all worthwhile. . . . Facing the risen Christ the disciples could now go out and do something about the problem of sin and suffering. They had seen the strong hands of God twist the crown of thorns into a crown of glory, and in hands as strong as that they knew themselves safe." The secret of facing any day's necessities with courage and honor is the strong faith of the Psalmist: "My God in his lovingkindness shall meet me." With the risen Christ, that faith becomes altogether persuasive. How does it come? Not by proof, arguments, or appeal to some tradition, but as Amos Wilder put it, ". . . this is a persuasion from within." If we go out to test this faith in all the circumstances of life, even in the "daily dust of life . . . no matter how low the ceiling under which we live, no matter how full of violence and menace, we will find an unbelievable, unaccountable irradiation of the dark places of our lives, a realization of the inexhaustible generosities of God at those precise points where there seem to be only irremediable evil and hopeless obstacles. . . .

"Light breaks where no sun shines."[5]

Robert Louis Stevenson, on one of his voyages to the South Seas, told about a terrific storm that frightened all the passengers. One man finally went out on deck and watched the captain pace the bridge, calm and undisturbed. He came back to the cabin

where the passengers were huddled together and said to them:
"I have seen the captain's face and all is well."

Suppose we find ourselves caught up in a total world war, a
struggle of life and death for the world that we know (assuming
here that such a struggle could end in anything but death for
all of us). We fight for a homeland that we love above every
other blessing, a kingdom where our families dwell, where love
has made us what we are, a kingdom where we have known peace,
justice, and opportunity, a kingdom of untold promise and benediction. Now part of the strategy of this war is to be liberation,
the liberation of lands and peoples from tyranny, from despotism,
and from slavery. This liberation of lands and peoples is a mission
of urgency, of danger and importance unparalleled in all the
strategies of this war. Our commander-in-chief must choose a
select company of soldiers for this operation. To them will be given
the finest training, the bravest leadership, the most precious
weapons and secrets of the kingdom. No sacrifice will be spared
to equip them and prepare them and support them in heart and
soul, in mind and body for the task given to them. Then, most
wonderful of all, the commander-in-chief himself will appear and
go with this company on the mission. He alone will go behind
enemy lines to perform the sacrifice that will breach the wall, that
will crack the defense and open the way for the company to follow. Now suppose we are chosen to do this thing. Suppose we are
picked by the American commander-in-chief. Suppose America
goes with us, her fortunes, her honor, the glories of her past, the
fears of her present, the hopes of her future. If this is true, how
will we feel? Humble, afraid, but with a steadiness and a readiness.
And there will be a loyalty that will subdue everything else; loyalty
born of gratitude for all the abundant mercies and gifts of the life
and land that we serve.

Now let us take this up above America—as far as imagination's
wings will carry us. *We have been chosen to do incredibly more
than that.* It is not America but the heavenly Kingdom for which

we fight. Our adversary is not another nation or alliance of nations but the principalities and powers, the hosts of wickedness. It is not the American commander-in-chief who has chosen us, but the King of the universe, if you can conceive of it. He has chosen us to be his own elect company in the liberation of the world from the tyranny of evil, from the despotism of fear, from the slavery of sin. Every sacrifice has been made to confirm us in this purpose and to prepare us for what we have to do. Our Lord and Master, the commander-in-chief if you will, has told us what we face—danger, suffering, death, even the death of this whole company. But he has told us he goes with us. He whose power conquered death and redeemed sin is with us at every step along the way, to fight with us, to lead us through all the way that he has gone and all the way that we must journey. This, nothing less than this, is what it means to have a risen Lord!

Easter, Pentecost, Trinity

The Wonderful Surprises of God

EASTER

C. S. LEWIS calls his autobiography *Surprised by Joy*. To Lewis, the astounding effect of the gospel, all unlooked for, when he finally received and accepted it, was the joy which he found in it. His title describes in three words the effect which the gospel has always had on people who received it. They have been surprised by the joy which they found. They have discovered that God is a God of wonderful surprises. The amazing, almost unbelievable consequence of trusting life to God is to find that He is able to do abundantly above all that we ask or even think. Always beyond our expectations, God is able to bring every equation into balance. Christian joy centers in the discovery that just when life has weighted the equation against us, God appears with astonishing power. He strikes victory into the heart of defeat. He lifts up hope out of despair. He gives healing for sin.

If I were to try to put the "Hallelujah" of Easter into one sentence, it would be this way: To everything that we and all the circumstances of life and death have put and can ever put into one side of the equation, God has shown that He is never less than equal on the other side. And this great surprise always comes at some appalling extremity—when life seems defeated beyond hope. Then God adds His measure, the measure that we and our timorous faith had not dared to count on, or even thought of, and everything is new again.

137

Of the numerous recognition scenes in the Bible, I think especially of three in which the wonderful, divine surprise came to someone who little expected it. When Joseph's brothers first hurled him into a deep pit and then sold him into slavery in Egypt, that was supposed to be the end of him. But it was not the end of Joseph. God had more for him to do. Later, when his astonished brothers, standing in the court of Pharaoh, recognized their brother Joseph, against whom they had executed all of this evil, Joseph said to them, "As for you, you meant evil against me, but God meant it for good." And it was good.

In the midst of someone's hopeless despair, God comes on with the same surprise of goodness and promise. We all know of someone or other with whom life has dealt harshly, as it did with Joseph—someone who has had to live at a disadvantage; someone physically or emotionally handicapped; someone exploited by others in a situation from which he had no escape. Joseph was made a slave, to live in exile from his home, his security at the mercy of an alien master. But he turned his limitations over to God and asked for God's help. We, too, can do what Joseph did. There is no situation that God cannot use in some way for good purpose, even slavery in Egypt. For in everything, God works for good with those who love Him. Even out of the discouraging evil impasse into which the world has come, God can do exceedingly abundantly. He can do all that we ask or think to bring forth good, for God is God, not man. God's purposes will prevail, and this faith enables and endows man with a glorious sense of freedom so that he can do what he must and endure what he must in the meantime.

In the New Testament we read another wonderful story of recognition: the story of a prodigal who went off into a far country and there squandered his life. And when he had wasted his all, he thought of his father's home and how even the hired help had more than he had, and he vowed to go back home again, not as a son, for he was not worthy of that, but as a serf. He started home laden with sin and full of remorse. But while yet a great way off, he was surprised by joy beyond his imagining, when his father ran to him, threw himself on his neck, and kissed him. Into the life of the prodigal who had sinned, God had come with the surprise of forgiveness. And so today, for him who is full of remorse, sick of his sins, wanting more than anything else to go home again, but not knowing how, there awaits the forgiving God. He is able to turn the darkness into light, that the prodigal may go home again.

Then there is that greatest recognition scene of all. Mary Magdalene, walking in the garden in despair, sees the gardener and asks him where they have taken her Lord. Jesus speaks one word, her name, "Mary," and the unbelievable surprise of the Resurrection floods over her soul.

Above all, into the loneliness and defeat left by death God comes with the surprise of the Resurrection. With all the diabolical force their imaginations could conjure up, men had tried to do away with the Saviour. They had humiliated him, stripped him of every last shred of decency and respect, and tortured him to a cruel death. As Peter later said at Pentecost, "This Jesus you crucified and killed by the hands of lawless men, but God raised him up, having loosed the pangs of death because it was not possible for him to be held by it." In death's dark vale we all must walk, but God walks with us. He is able to bear us across death's cold, sullen grief. Even as He marched through crucifixion to leave behind an empty tomb. God has prepared a surprise of triumph over our last enemy. On the one side suffering, but God on the other, while we are yet a great way off, sees us and redeems us. On the one side death, but God on the other raises us up. Hallelujah! Amen.

God with Us at Life's Lifting Places

PENTECOST

IT is reported in the Book of Acts that when Paul came to Ephesus he found some disciples there and asked them, "Did you receive the Holy Spirit when you believed?" The disciples answered, "No, we have never even heard that there is a Holy Spirit." Most of us are not in the same boat with the disciples. We have heard that there is a Holy Spirit. But great numbers of people today are genuinely confused by the idea of a Holy Spirit. What is it? they ask. God we know, and Christ we know, but who or what on earth is the Holy Spirit? Is it just a theological puzzle? Does it have any relevance to the common problems and universal needs of men? Puzzling as it is, the idea of the Holy Spirit is so central in Christian thought that one cannot readily detour around it or dismiss it with a shrug. And so men continue to wrestle with it hoping to get an answer.

It should be helpful to start by pointing out that the idea of the Holy Spirit came not out of the abstractions of some theologian's thinking but out of the experience of ordinary men. Ernest F. Scott has reminded us: "The early Christians did not invent the Holy Spirit. They knew they had received new energies, which must have come to them from above. . . . When they framed their belief in the Spirit, they were not just putting into words some abstract thinking, they were trying to explain visible facts which they could not account for in any other way." The Holy

140

Spirit was important to the early Christians because it accounted for the most important events and experiences in their lives. The reality of the Holy Spirit is no less important to us today. What we call it makes little difference as long as we don't miss it.

Let it be said clearly first of all to the person dubious about the doctrine or puzzled by the whole idea of the Holy Spirit, that the Holy Spirit is God. It need be no more complicated than that. Of course the Holy Spirit will always be mysterious as God Himself is mysterious, but just as we believe that God was in Christ, the divine Incarnation in human life, so we believe that God is in the Holy Spirit as the divine Power coming into our midst. In other words, the Holy Spirit is a way of describing something which God does. It's not just another name for God, but rather a description of something that God is doing, a description of God at work on earth in a particular way. What on earth is the Holy Spirit? is an unintentionally well-phrased question. The Holy Spirit is God engaged *on earth* in doing His work and His will.

It may be easy to understand the Holy Spirit if we can picture Him through analogy. The St. Lawrence Seaway is a system of navigation by which ships sail inland from the Atlantic Ocean to Lake Superior, rising over six hundred feet in the course of their voyage. The elevation is accomplished by a series of locks or lifting places where vessels are raised from lower to higher levels. At these lifting places where the rapids and waterfalls make river navigation impossible, the ships are lifted through canals of deep water. After the ship enters a lock, the lock is then flooded with water so that the boat rises to the level of the canal beyond the lock and can sail on at the higher altitude toward the destination far inland. Likewise, the Holy Spirit is God coming to our needs at the lifting places along the way of life's voyage, raising us from one level to another beyond rapids or breaking points where the journey would otherwise end.

First, we may think most commonly of the Holy Spirit as He comes with power and moving effect upon the Church. At how many lifting places has the Holy Spirit come to raise the Church up to where she could take new passages on her voyage! God came at Pentecost when the whole enterprise of His love and His will needed a forward move, a lifting up to new journeys. What would happen to the life, death, and resurrection of Christ now? Would this be just the death of one more prophet in Jerusalem, or would God use these events to gain new leverage upon men in the age-long struggle of love against hate, of good against evil, of light against the dark? In the outpouring of the Divine Spirit at Pentecost God came with power to lift the community of the covenant to new understandings and new enterprise. We can hardly tell at this distance what actually happened on that day, how many of the manifestations described in the Book of Acts appeared visibly and audibly, but that God lifted the whole undertaking of His will to new purposes and new dimensions no one can doubt.

The Holy Spirit moved upon the Church in the Reformation to lift her out of a suffocating ecclesiasticism and to carry her up steep passages in the river of years into new channels. Through Wycliffe, Luther, Calvin, Cranmer, Wesley, and their company the Church was led into ways more open to God's spirit. Men and women found the risen Lord to be an immediately present Power to judge, forgive, and redeem. Here was God entering the life of the Church in a new way, opening to men and women fresh resources: the Bible, the preaching of the Word, the mutual ministry among the whole community of the covenant.

In our own time the Holy Spirit has again moved on the whole Church, drawing many communions toward one ecumenical body. We are all one body in Christ; how then can Christ be divided? Where the Spirit has convicted us of our faithless divisions and moved us toward the one great communion of Christ—the holy Catholic Church—unsuspected Power has appeared to give forceful effect to the gospel, in places where its lifting power had never been tried or where it had long since been exhausted.

The Holy Spirit comes sometimes in a remarkable way to one particular congregation of Christians. Bryan Green tells of an industrial parish in England where the church had been lifeless and irrelevant to the necessities and concerns of her people. Then the Spirit of God began to possess that parish, lifting up first a few, then more and more men to witness for their faith. Green describes what happened in these words:

Each morning at six-thirty I met, for three-quarters of an hour, some sixty or seventy men and women of varying ages. Briefly I told them the main points of my sermon for that evening. For the next twenty minutes they put down in their notebooks, in their own words quite simply, any ideas they had about the subject about which I was going to preach. . . . Then we went round in turn reading what we had written down. . . . Out of the twenty or so contributions which we heard, six or seven would clearly fit in with the sermon. That evening before the service I met those particular contributors for half an hour of prayer and discussion. . . . After the worship in the service I preached the sermon. As soon as I had finished, I stayed in the pulpit while one after the other came up by me and had his say. . . . This cooperation was immensely powerful, and very many who would have been untouched by a sermon delivered by a clergyman were moved deeply by the preaching of the Word which came from the worshipping community. As one fine young worker put it when he told me that he had accepted Christ as his Saviour and King: "You see, Sir, it wasn't your sermon. It was what so-and-so said. He was one of us."[1]

Green reports what the vicar of that parish told him fifteen years later: "The Spirit of God had begun in the lives of men and women transformations which were still being completed within the life and membership of the church."

More than one congregation has been awakened to new life and new purpose by the Holy Spirit kindling upon them, arousing people out of moral lethargy to a dedication they had not known, or out of spiritual apathy to a discipline they had not accepted. It may not always happen as it happened in Green's industrial parish, but somewhere a congregation will discover a dedication or respond to a necessity and find both a rapture and a power which they had not known. God, by the sending forth of His own Spirit, seeks constantly to lift the Church to higher life. We believe He uses

all kinds of people, unimaginable situations, sometimes the queer-
est accidents of history, to reveal Himself and manifest His presence and His power. Henry P. Van Dusen has expressed it this
way: "The Holy Spirit testifies to the immediately present activity
of the Divine—God-near and God-mighty. The 'Spirit of God' or
'Holy Spirit' is always God-at-work."

We assume the right posture in thinking of God as the Supreme
Being, Majestic, Omnipotent; as the prophet Isaiah described
Him, "The High and Holy One who inhabits eternity." But we
must not forget the rest of what the prophet said: "Yet he makes
his dwelling with him who is of a contrite and humble spirit."
Just as Christ was the visible demonstration of the heart, mind, and
will of God for all the world to see, so the Holy Spirit is the man-
ifestation by which we are reminded that God is present, that He
is concerned, and that He is able for our immediate needs. To
speak in some orthodox terminology is not important. What is
of life-and-death consequence is that we do not lose the experience
of the Holy Spirit, that we do not unconsciously fall into ways of
thinking which put God far off and long ago, forgetting that He
is intimately present to His Church and to His people.

Second, it is no less true that the Holy Spirit comes to individuals at the decisive lifting places of life and bears them upward beyond breaking points in such a way that they do not
founder. Sometimes the Holy Spirit appears when least expected.
Sometimes life is lifted when we think it least likely we can avoid
shipwreck. The Holy Spirit came to one man in a pigpen once, a
man who had certainly made moral shipwreck of his life. But
God lifted the prodigal sinner up to the dignity of a forgiven
son and he was a new man. God stands close by to all our moral
defeats and failures so that if we "come to our selves" and ask his
forgiveness, we can stand up cleansed from all unrighteousness.

William Inge's play *The Dark at the Top of the Stairs* reveals
how the members of one family learn compassion, understanding,
and loving acceptance of each other through the suicide of a young
boy. As they recognize the hardness of their own hearts and their

part in this tragic breakdown, the evil dark is in some true measure redeemed. God stands close by to all our breakdowns that out of darkness His Holy Spirit might bring forth light. But what price redemption! When anyone cares deeply about life he cannot consent to the incredible price which evil demands, the staggering costs which our failures exact. Who can accept these without both wonder and rebellion? And before anyone chatters flippantly about the Holy Spirit's overcoming evil with good he ought to walk through the blighted slums of a great city and see the filth, the disease, the moral degradation which the Holy Spirit must overcome. Such redemption is not easily done, and it becomes us not to minimize the price to be paid. Yet beyond any question, the Holy Spirit can and does transform evil into love.

But, some will protest, if He can, why does it not always happen? One thinks of those words from Maxwell Anderson's *Winterset* where one embittered character says, "You talk of Jesus saving his lambs, I'll show you some lambs that Jesus forgot." Who can account for the forgotten "lambs"? It happens that life is not always put into the locks where God can lift it. Sometimes through its own tragic failure, sometimes through the evil and neglect of others, a life is so blighted, so denied, that it cannot receive God's lifting power. To know or to see such human derelicts ought to prompt the Christian to say of anyone who so deprived another life of its chance to be elevated above the breaking points what Jesus once said: "It were better for that man if he had a millstone hanged about his neck and were drowned in the midst of the sea."

Perhaps the most decisive lifting place at which the Holy Spirit ever meets a man is when He brings a person to renew a dedication to some high and holy purpose. When a man comes to some breaking point, unable to summon either strength or will to go on, then it is a matter of life and death to have his devotion restored, to discover a power that can keep him from sinking. We all come to such places of personal exhaustion, as the ship going up the St. Lawrence must come to the Lachine Rapids. Unless there be a canal with lifting locks to elevate that ship, she has reached her journey's end one thousand miles short of her destination. In the life of the soul, unless there be some lifting power where its own consecration runs out, it cannot reach beyond the rapids. And there are vast numbers of people in the middle stages of life who have come to these rapids. Their commitment is all played out. But here the Holy Spirit does meet them to lift them if they will let Him.

God works through beauty to refresh tired spirits. Many would testify to the healing power of music, or art, or literature. James Weldon Johnson tells of how his soul was once transfigured for a spell by the soaring music of Wagner's Prelude to *Lohengrin*, which he heard in a Berlin opera house. It gave inspiration in the strength of which he could abide the savage humiliation that came to him that same night on account of his dark skin. Many would confirm from personal experience the report of Wordsworth on the effect of nature on his soul: "I have felt a presence that disturbs me with the joy of elevated thoughts." Dedication is often renewed by great beauty.

But where the Holy Spirit's lifting is of even greater consequence is not in the presence and effect of things naturally and inherently beautiful but in the presence of things naturally ugly and inherently evil. Here is where a man needs a mighty lift if he is to go on, when all the circumstances are set to pull him under and destroy him. It is at this point that God draws a man up by the inspiration of great dedication, when the thing toward which life is set outpulls the drag and drowning effect of disappointment and frustration. This is God working through the circumstances of life and the emotions of human feeling.

Robert Louis Stevenson's life brought him about as much misery as ten men are usually required to suffer in a lifetime: illness, pain, misunderstanding. Again and again he was down in the depths of misery and almost hopeless prospect, yet always he could say, "There is something in me worth saying." It was the worth of what could be done that saved him. Compounded though his devotion surely was with personal ambition; having little that one could identify with "religious" consecration; nevertheless, this dedication to moral goodness and to human blessedness was a power that sustained and elevated Stevenson at a long succession of lifting places. In the face of every kind of affliction he had, according to one biographer, a "courage that did not even bother to be grim." As Stevenson once wrote to Meredith:

For fourteen years I have not had a day's real health; I have wakened sick and gone to bed weary; and I have done my work unflinchingly. I have written in bed, and written out of it, written in hemorrhages, written in sickness, written torn by coughing, written when my head swam for weakness; . . . I am better now, have been rightly speaking since first I came to the Pacific; and still, few are the days when I am not in some physical distress. And the battle goes on—ill or well, is a trifle; so as it goes. I was made for a contest, and Powers have willed that my battlefield should be this dingy, inglorious one of the bee and the physic bottle. . . . I would have preferred a place of trumpetings and the open air over my head.[2]

The great author of *Kidnapped* and *Treasure Island* perhaps would not have called it God's Spirit. The eyes of faith, however, may recognize God at Stevenson's lifting places, and may recognize God where countless others have been lifted up in dedication to making the world a more blessed place in which to dwell.

The eyes of faith will recognize God at their own personal lifting places when the going is impossible under their own power. God meets the Church when she is bound and cannot move. God waits where His holy purposes need the Divine lift. God waits where each of us needs Him most. The Second Isaiah gives us this promise from God: "Even to your old age I am He, and to gray hairs I will carry you. I have made, and I will bear; I will carry and will save." This is a text to give faith and comfort when the going is steep, to set alongside those words from the New Testament: "The Holy Spirit, whom the Father will send in my name, He shall teach you all things."

Saint Bernard, according to Donald Baillie, told his monks that however early they might wake and rise for prayer in their chapel on a cold midwinter morning, or even in the dead of night, they would always find God awake before them, waiting for them— "nay, it was He that had awakened them to seek His face." This is what faith tells us about the Holy Spirit, that He is waiting for us at every place where we need to be lifted. Dr. Van Dusen includes us all when he points to our deepest needs. For some of us our primary need is for physical reinforcement in hours of weakness; for some it is for moral strength to master temptation and transcend failure. Or our need may be for guidance in personal perplexity and confusion, or for cleansing and remaking in the despair of devastating self-knowledge, or for the basic essentials of character. And for all of us our most urgent necessity is for the fruits of the spirit: love, joy, peace, patience, kindness, goodness, faithfulness, gentleness, self-control. In every one of these needs God waits for us with a steadying arm for our weakness, with restraining force for our temptations, with the spirit of truth for our perplexities, with forgiveness for our sins. May it be that God's Holy Spirit will meet each one in his own frightful needs with His resources to confirm and claim us for Himself, that we may be borne ahead toward our high calling in Jesus Christ.

God's Three Ways of Being God

TRINITY

FEW if any hymns are more sung in Protestant worship than this one:

> Holy, holy, holy! Lord God Almighty!
> Early in the morning our song shall rise to thee;
> Holy, holy, holy! merciful and mighty!
> God in Three Persons, blessed Trinity!

At least twice each Sunday the congregation gives voice to its faith in the Trinity. The Gloria Patri begins, "Glory be to the Father, and to the Son, and to the Holy Ghost." The Doxology ends, "Praise Father, Son and Holy Ghost." And the most often repeated benediction is that of Paul from II Corinthians: "The grace of the Lord Jesus Christ, the love of God, and the fellowship of the Holy Spirit, be with you all."

Father, Son, and Holy Spirit—the three "persons" of the Trinity. To take away any part of this formula from our faith or worship would be to mutilate our spiritual life. Christian faith could not sustain the amputation of any side of this triangle. Yet how many of us really understand what those words mean and why we use them? Our ignorance and bewilderment are not surprising. For more than fifteen centuries the Trinity has been the most controversial doctrine and the thorniest problem in all of Christian thought. Even Thomas Aquinas felt obliged to leave the matter in some such way as this: "The Trinity is a holy mystery." Moreover, a great deal of the talk has *seemed*, at least, to be pathetically in-

149

consequential—theological hairsplitting. For this reason, mention of the Trinity to many people provokes neither devotion nor antagonism, but rather a vast indifference. Who would be aroused by the anticipation of a sermon on the Trinity?

Commonly, there are two impediments in this affair. First, the idea of the Trinity is complex and difficult to understand. Second, what difference would it make if we did understand it? "Why make this so needlessly complicated?" people ask. "Would it not be better just to say that God is one, and leave it at that?" Some people think it clever to spoof the doctrine of the Trinity. "How can you say that 1 plus 1 plus 1 equals 1, when any fool knows that 1 plus 1 plus 1 equals 3?" Trinity Sunday brings at least the challenge to meet some of the difficulties in our minds, and to suggest why this doctrine is important, why we do not give it up, and what difference it makes to your life and mine.

We begin by saying that the Trinity is the very center of our faith; it is the formula by which we describe the Way, the Truth, the Life of Christian experience. Why? *Because we can't say all we ought to say about God unless we talk of Him as a Trinity.* I think we may be able to see it best by an analogy: We can't say all that ought to be said about American government unless we talk of the three branches. To speak only of the Presidency, or only of the Congress, or only of the Judiciary, and ignore either or both of the other branches would be to give but a fragmentary description of our government. So in talking of God, to speak only of God as Father and Creator, and to say nothing of God as we see Him in Jesus Christ our Lord and Saviour, or as we know Him in the Holy Spirit, would be to fail completely to describe God. Because in these matters an answer that is one-half or one-third right is *all* wrong!

I suppose many people are under the impression that the Trinity is an idea that was "hatched up" by the Church fathers in the early centuries during those Church councils when Christian faith was articulated and formalized into creeds. This is *not* the case any more than that the Constitution of the United States with its threefold way of government was "hatched up" by the founding fathers out of the theories of Jefferson, Madison, and Franklin. We have a threefold pattern of government because the realities of political life and the facts of early American experience made it clear to those statesmen that, except with a trinitarian structure of government, a democracy in all likelihood would fail. Likewise, *the idea of the Trinity appeared because men somehow had to explain their experience.* They couldn't account for it in any other way. The experience, the facts of God came first; then the creed, the doctrine, the worship. When Paul wrote his threefold benediction to the Corinthians he had never heard of the doctrine of the Trinity, nor would anyone else hear of it for 250 years. What Paul was praying was that the fullness of God's blessing would be upon the Corinthians, and if they were to know God in all His fullness, they would know Him through the grace of the Lord Jesus Christ, through the love of God the Father, and through the fellowship of the Holy Spirit. As Karl Barth has helpfully stated it: "The Trinity is a description of God's three ways of being God."

Perhaps it would help further if we understood more exactly what the Church means when it speaks of God in "Three Persons." The word "person" here does not mean the same thing that we have in mind when we speak of each other as persons. It derives from the Latin word *persona*, which was widely used in the theater of classical Greece and Rome. *Persona* indicated the mask put on by the actors in order to play different parts, and the word was taken over by the early theologians to express the *diverse forms of God's activity*, without destroying the concept of His unity. I wish sometimes we might have another word than "persons," since it frequently suggests three Gods. We will more nearly approach the truth if we always think of it as one God in three aspects, three ways—truly *ways* in which God is present, not just phenomena that point to God.

First, let us look more closely at the Trinity, and begin where Christian experience has always begun—not at the beginning with the Father, but in the middle with *God the Son*. This is where

Paul begins his benediction—"The grace of the Lord Jesus Christ."
In Christ we meet God face to face. "He that hath seen me hath
seen the Father." "The Father is in me." These are Jesus' own
words about himself. When they were remembered by the disciples in later times, and in the light of the cross and the Resurrection, the realization grew that their Jesus whom they had known
and loved was no less than God Himself. So Peter cried at Pentecost: "God has made him both Lord and Christ, this Jesus whom
you crucified." So Paul wrote to the Corinthians, "God was in
Christ reconciling the world unto himself." So the writer of the
Fourth Gospel put it, "God so loved the world that he gave his
only begotten Son." This was *God* whom the disciples met. This
was *God* whom Paul met as the risen Christ on the Damascus
Road. And whenever men have met Him and found themselves
set free from sin, found themselves to be new creatures, delivered
from the bondage of fear, they have been sure that they were
meeting God Almighty.

Someone's mind, however, is running ahead and has come up
with the big question. Let me put it to you as one boy asked it of
a teacher who was trying to tell him about the Trinity. "Well, if
Christ was God," he said, "how could God be ruling in heaven
while He was living as a man in Palestine? And who was ruling
over the universe during those thirty years?" How would we answer
the boy? It is the central question. *If God was in Christ*, then who
"took over" for God in the role of Creator and Everlasting Lord?

Now it's no good saying that God was not really in Christ. The
experience which his followers had of Christ convinced them that
God must have been in Christ to account for what happened. God
must have been there in a way that He was not found in any other
life. Stephen Neill put it in these words of vivid contrast:

The Christian's God loved the world so much that He entered into
the world, and was willing to live among men as Man. If you say that
God was not really in Christ any more than He is in any other man,
then you imply that God *did not* love the world enough to enter into
it and to live among men as Man. To say that God was in Christ is

to say that *God knows by experience* what it is to be betrayed, unjustly condemned, insulted, crucified, buried. To say that God was not in Christ is to imply that God *does not* know by experience what it means to suffer all those things. To say that God was in Christ is to say that God knows *by experience* what it is to be tired and hungry, sorrowful and lonely. To believe as do many who deny the Trinity, is to say that God may understand by *sympathy*, but that He does not know *by experience* what it is to be tired and hungry, sorrowful and lonely.[1]

Consider the parallel. A whole nation rejoiced and wept recently as we shared sympathetically in the reunion of four American fliers with their families after two years in Communist prisons. We can all imagine something of what they went through during two years of imprisonment, brain-washing, and punishment. But none of us really knows what life was for those gallant aviators. We were not there. We've had no experience to match theirs. Is that the way it is with God and ourselves? Christian faith says no! We say that God was here in this prison with us. He knows your life and mine *from experience.* How else could there truly be a *grace of the Lord Jesus Christ?* This is one of God's ways of being God!

Second, being sure that God was in Christ, and seeing the kind of God who was in Jesus, the only answer we can give to the boy's question is to say that God was and is also *a great love* at the heart of creation: "Love divine, all loves excelling." This is God. Through Jesus Christ we see a God who is loving Father—almost as though we saw through a window into the heart of the universe. On account of the grace of Christ we know God, no longer as mere Judge, or Lawgiver, or Creator, but as heavenly Father.

Donald Baillie has said that "the most remarkable fact in the whole history of religious thought is this: that when the early Christians looked back and pondered on the dreadful thing that had happened, it made them think of the redeeming love of God. Not simply the love of Jesus, *but the love of God.*"

This is what happens: Because through Christ we know that love is on God's throne, (1) frustration cannot limit a man's life,

(2) perplexities cannot bring despair, (3) persecution cannot make us outcast, (4) depression cannot break our spirit. The man who knows that he is loved by God can never be defeated by life. "Yes, in all things we are more than conquerors." For neither death nor life, nor things present nor things to come, nor height nor depth, nor anything else in all creation shall separate us from "*the love of God*." God's second way of being God.

Third, we still haven't said all we mean by God until we say "*God the Holy Spirit*." This is the way James Stewart once summed it up:

> You may believe in the Father—God immortal, invisible, eternal and transcendent, beyond the bounds of time and history. You may believe in the Son—God manifest in the flesh, dramatically breaking through into the temporal and historic. But what you need to bring all this home to you yourself, to make it valid and effective and personal in daily living, is not only God in the eternities, or God in history,— *it is God in you, making your heart His dwelling place.*

This is what makes it all relevant to us. God present with us and in us. Not just the Lord of Creation, not just One who walked the earth nineteen centuries ago, but One to whom we pray this morning: "Spirit of God, descend upon my heart." Pentecost, with the outpouring of God's self upon the fellowship which became His Church; the conversion experiences, all the way from Paul to people who confess Christ as Lord and Saviour in our midst in new Pentecosts—all of this has been unassailable evidence that God is with us, not only as Truth in our minds, but as kindling Spirit in our hearts. *This is God's third way of being God!* One God in Three Persons—three ways.

If I may be permitted to draw an analogy from my own experience, it might help not only to clarify this concept but also to show how anyone can demonstrate it to himself with reference to his own life.

I first knew my father as a person of flesh and blood. He was the man of our house. There was a special relationship between us. He mysteriously disappeared in the morning, returned at night.

For many years I had no clear notion of what he did; in some way or other I understood it to be "work," and that his "work" took care of me and the others in the family. I knew my father first as a man who lived with me, played with me, worked with me, taught me, loved me.

Then as I grew up I understood that my father was more than just *my father*. He had a wider work to do than just take care of me. He had a mission to fulfill in the world. I was part of his work and mission; I belonged to his love and concern equally with all the other members of my father's home. But his work and mission in the world was greater than I. It included more than me. I realized that my father was here before I came. In fact, he created me. He created me not only biologically but in love. In his action was loving purpose: to create a home where he could be loved and where he could love all of his family. His intention was to create an environment in which we could grow to share his love and his concerns. Father became more than just the man called Daddy, more than just the man who saved me from trouble. I knew him as creator, the author of a whole realm of life and purpose that included me.

Then came the day when I went away to school to study for the ministry. I left home, so to speak, so that my father was no longer with me in the flesh. But then it was that I found he could be with me in his spirit. Something of his spirit, his will, his love went with me. An even more wonderful thing happened. No longer with me as a man in the flesh, now that I was doing his work—in a manner of speaking I was following in his way, coming to know the great things he had long ago learned, doing the things which he had long mastered to perfection, loving the work which he loved—now that I was doing his work which was also my work, I discovered more of his heart and mind and spirit than I had ever known before. In my commitment to his own great work, in my reading of his books, in my study of the great way on which we both had set to walk, I found a meeting with his spirit that made all things new, even the familiar things of old acquaintance.

Now, of course, in all of this picture I am talking about just one man, not three. But I can't possibly say all that ought to be said about my father except as I describe his three ways of being himself. I know him as creator, creator of a whole world of ideas and plans and purposes of which I was one part. I know him as a man, in a person-to-person relationship, the incarnation and witness to his real self which no eye hath seen. I know him as a spirit, as a living person in my own heart. To leave my father out as creator would rob my life of any meaning or purpose (quite aside from the unlikelihood of my being here at all). To leave him out as a man, earthy, able to know me, would make it impossible for me ever to know the wonderful love and will of his soul which has to be expressed in a life. To leave him out as spirit would reduce the whole thing to a fleeting affair of the moment, then to be gone.

This analogy is imperfect; don't try to press it any farther than it will readily go. But it does suggest Trinity—three real persons in one unity. Trinity is a way of describing vital relationships. You can't know God in any of His ways without knowing Him in the other two. And you see what it all means and what a difference it makes:

God the Father: We are children of a Love divine, whose souls belong to the heart of the eternal who is a Father, most wonderfully kind.

God the Son: God has come down into the midst of darkest valleys to contend with us against every evil thing, and to keep us from falling, and to present us faultless before His own presence.

God the Holy Spirit: We are not alone, no matter where we go or what befalls us. God the Holy Spirit, the Comforter, abides with us forever.

Notes

Chapter I *When the Best We Have Is Not Enough*
1. From *The Autobiography of J. Middleton Murry.*
2. Rufus Jones, *The Luminous Trail* (New York: The Macmillan Company, 1947).
3. T. S. Eliot, *Murder in the Cathedral*, Part I. *The Complete Poems and Plays of T. S. Eliot* (New York: Harcourt, Brace and Company, Inc., 1952), p. 195. Used by permission.

Chapter II *God Helps Those Who Cannot Help Themselves*
1. J. Colwell, in *Great Texts of the Bible*, ed. by James Hastings (New York: Charles Scribner's Sons, 1914), Matthew, p. 9.

Chapter III *God's Gift to a World That Has Everything*
1. John Masefield, *The Coming of Christ* (New York: The Macmillan Company, 1928), pp. 26–32.
2. Norman Cousins, in *The United Church Herald*, Nov. 20, 1958.
3. Arthur C. Clarke, in *The New York Times Magazine*, Nov. 30, 1958.

Chapter IV *In a Raveled World, Love Endures*
1. Robert Gorham Davis, in *The New York Times Book Review*, Dec. 26, 1954.
2. Norman Cousins, in *The Saturday Review*, Oct. 29, 1955.
3. Morris Bishop, in *The New Yorker*, May 25, 1955. Used by permission.
4. Phyllis McGinley, *Love Letters* (New York: The Viking Press, 1954). Used by permission.

157

Chapter V   *Life Fashioned in the Style of Christ*

1. Peter Bertocci, *Religion As Creative Insecurity* (New York: Association Press, 1958), p. xiii.

2. Albert Edward Bailey, *The Gospel in Art* (Boston: Pilgrim Press, 1916), p. 261.

Chapter VI   *Our Exceeding Need and God's Exceeding Love*

1. T. S. Eliot, *The Cocktail Party. The Complete Poems and Plays of T. S. Eliot* (New York: Harcourt, Brace and Company, 1952), p. 342. Used by permission.

2. Sir Arnold Toynbee, *An Historian's Approach to Religion* (New York: Oxford Press, 1956), p. 24.

3. Henri Barbusse, *Under Fire,* Everyman's Library Edition (New York: E. P. Dutton and Co., 1928). Cited in *The Grandeur and Misery of Man* by David Roberts (New York: Oxford Press, 1955), p. 155.

4. Alec Vidler, *Christian Belief* (New York: Charles Scribner's Sons, 1950), p. 96.

Chapter VII   *Conversation with God in His Own Tongue*

1. Stephen Vincent Benét, *A Minor Litany,* from *The Selected Works of Stephen Vincent Benét* (New York: Rinehart and Co., Inc., 1942). Used by permission.

2. Walter de la Mare, *The Listeners,* from *The Collected Poems of Walter de la Mare* (New York: Henry Holt and Co., 1920), p. 144. Used by permission.

3. Ellen Glasgow, *Vein of Iron* (New York: Harcourt, Brace and Company, 1935).

4. Source unknown.

Chapter VIII   *For Life Dispersed on Ribbon Roads*

1. Robert Nisbet, *The Quest for Community* (New York: Oxford University Press, 1953), p. 10.

2. T. S. Eliot, *Choruses from "The Rock"* in *The Complete Poems and Plays of T. S. Eliot* (New York: Harcourt, Brace and Company, 1952), p. 101. Used by permission.

3. Dan Jacobson, in *The Reporter,* Feb. 21, 1957.

4. Amos Wilder, *Modern Poetry and the Christian Tradition* (New York: Charles Scribner's Sons, 1952), p. 229.

5. Bertram Beck, in *The Saturday Review*, Sept. 11, 1954.

6. John Masefield, *The Seekers. The Collected Poems of John Masefield* (London: W. Heinemann Ltd., 1932).

Chapter IX   *Long Night's Journey into Day*

1. John Masefield, *In the Mill* (New York: The Macmillan Company, 1941), p. 16.

2. Amy Loveman, in *The Saturday Review*, Sept. 18, 1954.

Chapter X   *For Such a King We've Waited All Our Life*

1. Warren Weaver, in *Look*, Dec. 24, 1957.

2. Edwin Hodder, *The Life and Work of the 7th Earl of Shafts- bury* (New York: Cassell & Co., Vol. 2, 1886), p. 50.

Chapter XI   *Living in Two Worlds at Once*

1. John S. Whale, *The Christian Faith* (London: Student Christian Movement Press, 1938), p. 77.

2. Sir Arnold Toynbee, quoted in *Third Church Messenger*, Rochester, N. Y., Jan. 14, 1955.

3. Mary Ellen Chase, *The White Gate* (New York: W. W. Norton, 1954), p. 97.

4. Quoted in *The Gates of New Life* by James S. Stewart (New York: Charles Scribner's Sons, 1938), p. 244.

5. Amos Wilder, *Otherworldliness and the New Testament* (New York: Harper & Brothers, 1954), p. 64.

Chapter XIII   *God with Us at Life's Lifting Places*

1. Bryan Green, *The Practice of Evangelism* (New York: Charles Scribner's Sons, 1951), p. 57.

2. Joseph C. Furnas, *Voyage to Windward* (New York: William Sloane Associates, 1951).

Chapter XIV   *God's Three Ways of Being God*

1. Stephen Neill, *The Christian's God* (New York: Association Press, 1955), p. 80.